THE Project Management Tool Kit

THE Project Management Tool Kit

100 TIPS AND TECHNIQUES FOR GETTING THE JOB DONE RIGHT

Tom Kendrick

American Management Association
New York | Atlanta | Brussels | Chicago
Mexico City | San Francisco | Shanghai
Tokyo | Toronto | Washington, D. C.

Special discounts on bulk quantities of AMACOM books are available to corporations, professional associations, and other organizations. For details, contact Special Sales Department, AMACOM, a division of American Management Association, 1601 Broadway, New York, NY 10019.
Tel.: 212-903-8316. Fax: 212-903-8083.
Web site: www. amacombooks.org

This publication is designed to provide accurate and authoritative information in regard to the subject matter covered. It is sold with the understanding that the publisher is not engaged in rendering legal, accounting, or other professional service. If legal advice or other expert assistance is required, the services of a competent professional person should be sought.

Library of Congress Cataloging-in-Publication Data

Kendrick, Tom.
   The project management tool kit : 100 tips and techniques for getting the job done right / Tom Kendrick.
      p.   cm.
"Includes processes from all of the areas outlined in the Project Management Institute (PMI) PMBOK® Guide, 2000 Edition"—P.   .
Includes index.
      ISBN 0-8144-0810-9
   1. Project management—Outlines, syllabi, etc.   I. Project Management Institute.   II. Guide to the project management body of knowledge (PMBOK guide.   III. Title.
HD69.P75K462 2000
658.4′04—dc22   2003023995

Printing number

10 9 8 7 6 5 4 3 2

To my family:

My father, Tom Kendrick,
his father, also Tom Kendrick,
and my uncle, George Kendrick.
They taught me the value of tools and logic.

My wife, Barbara Kendrick, for her support and
tireless work ensuring this book was coherent.

Contents

How to Use This Book (Read This First!)

If you are typical of others leading projects today, you are very busy. Time pressures, complexity of project work, and lack of sufficient resources make your work challenging and difficult. Successful project management requires you to execute efficiently and well, even in situations where you may have little experience.

The Project Management Tool Kit assembles short, easy-to-apply summaries of proven project management practices. These concise summaries will help you achieve consistently better results in your projects. Novice project leaders will be able to apply the process steps as a *roadmap* to understand what is necessary in unfamiliar situations. Experienced managers can use the process summaries as a *checklist* to ensure that they do not leave out anything essential, especially when a project requires something out of the ordinary.

NOTE: The processes in *The Project Management Tool Kit* are arranged in alphabetical order. To facilitate skimming, within each process keywords are in *italics,* and cross-references to related processes elsewhere in the book are **boldface.**

The Project Management Tool Kit is based on established, practical ideas used by successful project managers in many fields, and includes processes from all of the areas outlined in the Project Management Institute (PMI) *PMBOK® Guide, 2000 Edition.* Like any good reference book *The Project Management Tool Kit* is organized for quick, *random* access to process guidance. The purpose of this book is to arrange the fundamental processes of project management in an easy-to use, compact format.

All projects are different, so each will undoubtedly require additional processes, beyond those included here, to deal with unique challenges. While not every project will need all of the practices in this book, most will prove useful, particularly after you make the minor adjustments necessary to customize them to your specific environment.

A casual reader may want to begin by reading the *highest-level* processes of **Project Plan Development** and **Project Plan Execution** (Chapters 61 and 62). The processes in this book may also be grouped in the *specific categories* that follow. In the PMI© PMBOK®, the nine knowledge areas are numbered 4 through 12. The first four categories in this book include processes from PMBOK® knowledge area 4 (Project Integration Management), as well as additional project management processes of a more general nature. Categories 5 through 12 directly map to knowlege areas 5 through 12 of the PMBOK®. These lists will serve you as an index to related practices and concepts, in a typical sequence of application.

THE Project Management Tool Kit

1 **Activity Definition** (PMBOK® 6.1)

WHAT: Documenting the activities resulting from the lowest level of the project work breakdown structure (WBS) and assigning an owner to each.

WHEN: Project planning.

RESULTS: Clear descriptions of all identified project work and delegation of responsibility.

Verify Activities

Activity definition is a key step in **project plan development.** After developing the work breakdown structure as part of **scope definition,** verify that all work listed is *necessary.* If the work at the lowest level will probably require more than a month to complete or consume more than 80 hours of effort, strive to break it down further.

Work related to organizational, business, or legal requirements is often overlooked. Examples include preparation for life-cycle checkpoints, methodology requirements, project and other reviews, scheduled presentations, and specific documents the project must create. Add any *missing work* you discover to the plan.

Describe Activities

Convert the lowest-level WBS entries into project activities that can be estimated, scheduled, and tracked. Check that each represents a *discrete,* separate piece of work that has a start and a stop point. For each piece of work, capture and document any assumptions.

Describe each lowest-level work package concisely in terms of the work to be done and the task deliverable (examples: install power, edit user documentation). These *verb-noun descriptions* ensure clarity and make planning and tracking easier.

Identify one or more specific *deliverables* for each lowest-level activity. For each deliverable, specify the acceptance or test criteria. Be able to describe any requirements relating to standards, performance, or specific quality level. If the deliverable for an activity cannot be clearly defined, the work may be unnecessary; consider deleting it.

Assign Owners

Seek capable, motivated owners for each lowest-level activity. Staff all work possible using *willing volunteers,* and remember that the project leader remains responsible for all tasks without an owner.

For each activity, assign one and only *one owner,* **delegating responsibility** for the work. Owners will be responsible for planning, estimating, monitoring, and reporting on the activity, but will not necessarily do all the work alone. In some cases, owners will lead a team doing the work, or even serve as liaisons for outsourced tasks. For each activity, identify all needed skills, staff, and any other resources.

Document Activities

Document all activities in a database, **software tool for project management,** or some other appropriate format. Include activity names, owners, assumptions, deliverable descriptions, and other important information. The activity list (sometimes called a *WBS Dictionary*) serves as the foundation for project planning, risk analysis, execution, and control. Provide all activity owners a list of their work.

Use activity definitions as a foundation for many other planning processes, including **activity duration estimating, activity sequencing, cost estimating, risk identification, required skills analysis,** and **responsibility analysis.**

As the project planning and execution proceed, keep activity information current. Periodically *update* the activity list to add work identified during the project.

2 Activity Duration Estimating (PMBOK® 6.3)

WHAT: Forecasting durations for all identified project activities.

WHEN: Project planning, execution, and control.

RESULTS: Duration estimates in workdays for all project tasks.

Determine Duration

Duration estimates are a central component of **project plan development.** For each listed task in your project **activity definition,** use **responsibility analysis** and other planning data to develop *timing estimates,* in workdays. Useful estimating ideas include:

➤ *History* (**lessons learned,** databases of **project diagnostic metrics**)

➤ *Activity owner analysis* and personal experience

➤ *Analogs* (previous work of a similar type)

➤ *Experts* (consultants, peers, managers, vendor proposals)

➤ *Published data* (WWW, papers, articles, professional magazines)

➤ *Parametric or size-based formulas* ("rules of thumb;" complexity analysis; component or module counts; function points and other code assessments; measurements of volume, area, length, or other parameters)

➤ *Team analysis* (**Delphi technique,** further work decomposition)

If duration estimates exceed your standards for length (twenty workdays is a typical maximum), consider further decomposition. Update the project *work breakdown structure* from **scope definition** to reflect any changes you make.

Refine Duration Estimates and Reconcile with Effort Estimates

Refine the initial duration estimates using factors specific to your project such as:

➤ Project *constraints and assumptions*

➤ Any unclear *project specifications* from **scope planning**

➤ Any known delays or requirements for synchronization of work from **activity sequencing**

➤ Probable *scope changes*

➤ Technical *complexity*

➤ Requirements for *unusually high* reliability or performance

➤ Overall *project length*

➤ Requirements for *innovation,* investigation, or invention

➤ *Training*

Duration and effort estimates (from **cost estimation**) are closely linked. Which you do first for project planning does not matter much, but reconcile them before finalizing a baseline plan. Adjust any estimates of duration to *ensure consistency* with your effort analysis.

Consider Risks and Alternatives

Once you have made a "most likely" duration estimate, probe for failure modes and potential problems. Determine the timing consequences of *worst cases.*

You may adjust estimates for uncertainty using the *PERT* (Program Evaluation and Review Technique) formula: $t_e = (t_o + 4t_m + t_p)/6$, where t_e is a weighted average "expected" duration, based on t_o: an optimistic duration, t_m: the most likely duration, and t_p: a pessimistic duration.

For estimates in which you have low confidence, seek alternative ways of performing the work that rely on older, more *established methods* that can be estimated more accurately.

Capture the Duration Data

Document duration estimates in workdays to use in **schedule development.** Duration estimates are the principal estimates used by **software tools for project management,** and a schedule database is a standard place to store them.

Revise duration estimates as needed to resolve timing problems during the project through **schedule control.**

Revalidate estimates periodically during **project reviews,** particularly for lengthy projects.

3 Activity Sequencing (PMBOK® 6.2)

WHAT: Determining dependencies between project activities.

WHEN: Project planning.

RESULTS: A graphical or tabular summary of project work flow.

Review Project Data

Activity sequencing is generally done in parallel with **activity duration estimating** during **project plan development.** Sequencing is a *bottom-up planning* process, not based on fixed-date or arbitrarily imposed, top-down deadlines. Significant plan variances against project timing objectives are best resolved through **constraint management and plan optimization** and **negotiating project changes.**

To begin, assemble project **activity definitions,** along with other *project information,* such as organizational standards, life-cycle and methodology requirements, constraints, and assumptions.

Milestones

In addition to project activities, which consume time and effort, project schedules also have milestones—*moments in time* having no duration used to synchronize project work and to mark significant transitions in the project. Uses for milestones include:

➤ Project start

➤ Project end

➤ Completion of related parallel activities

➤ Phase gates or life-cycle stage transitions

➤ Significant decisions, approvals, or events

➤ Interfaces between **multiple dependent projects**

➤ Other external activity dependencies and deliverables

List all project milestones.

Identify Dependencies

There are many ways to *model project work flow,* but the easiest and most effective is to build an activity network using activity and milestone descriptions written on yellow sticky notes arrayed on a large piece of paper (or wall) where they can be moved around readily. This manual "activity on node" analysis (also called precedence diagramming) has several advantages over alternative approaches:

➤ It is easier to do as a team than to enter dependency data directly into a computer scheduling tool.

➤ Dependency analysis on a small computer screen can be confusing, so it is easy to miss critical linkages.

➤ Other approaches, such as "activity on arrow," are less intuitive for most people, and they are not consistent with standard **software tools for project management,** where the information developed will likely be stored.

Starting from the initial milestone, begin linking the activities and milestones, based on logical work flow and use of the activities' deliverables. There are several *linkage types* that represent virtually all project dependencies:

➤ **Finish-to-Start:** Work is sequential. The first activity must be done before one or more following activities can begin. This linkage is most common; it is the default in project scheduling tools.

➤ **Start-to-Start:** Work is synchronized. This type of linkage occurs when work must start and progress simultaneously.

➤ **Finish-to-Finish:** Activity deliverables are synchronized. Finish-to-finish links are most common whenever the task deliverables may change or deteriorate if not used promptly.

➤ **Start-to-Finish:** The initiation of work on an activity forces the termination of an earlier activity. Real requirements for this are very rare.

Lags and leads may also be modeled, by defining an offset in time between activities. They may be Finish-to-Start, Finish-to-Finish, or Start-to-Start.

Because a project network is a model of work flow through time, linkages (the arrows used to connect the activities and milestones) *must not loop* back on themselves. If rework is required, define additional new activities. Scheduling software checks for and will not permit loops.

Document Project Work Sequences

Check that each activity and milestone is linked backward to at least one predecessor (except for the initial milestone) and forward to at least one successor (except for the final milestone). Ensure *continuity of workflow* on each path in the network. If you find logical gaps where you are missing work

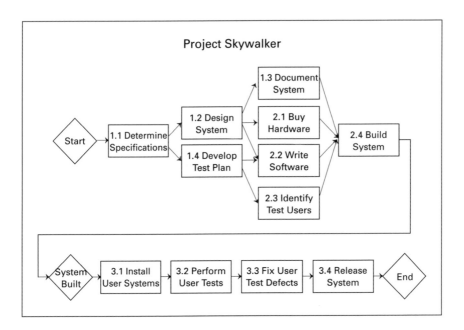

Project Skywalker

necessary to connect defined activities, describe it and add it to the work breakdown structure of your **scope definition.**

Use the *graphical representation* of the project to support **schedule development** and critical path analysis. Some other names for this network diagram are:

➤ Logical project networks

➤ PERT charts (Although true Program Evaluation and Review Technique charts are actually different, this usage has become common.)

➤ Dependency diagrams

If you intend to use scheduling software to assist in managing your project, *enter the dependency data* from your network chart into the tool's database.

Revalidate dependencies between activities periodically during **project reviews,** especially on lengthy projects.

4 **Administrative Closure** (PMBOK® 10.4)

WHAT: Completion of project management tasks at the end of a project.

WHEN: Project closure.

RESULTS: Final project documents and project lessons learned.

Formal Acceptance

Review **scope planning** and your records of **scope change control** to determine the project *deliverable requirements*. Check that all final testing is aligned with the agreed-upon specifications.

Work with the people who must evaluate your project results to complete **scope verification,** formally acknowledging that the project deliverable has met the project goals. If there are no issues, get *formal sign-off* from your project sponsor, and as appropriate from customers or other stakeholders. For projects undertaken for a fee, ensure the customer is properly and promptly billed.

If the project fails to deliver on some objectives, obtain written acknowledgement of the *partial results* that were delivered. Even when **canceling projects,** formally document all accomplishments.

Final Project Documentation

Whatever the ultimate result of the project may be, *write a report* to summarize results and to acknowledge contributors. This report is generally similar in format to project **performance reporting.** Use the report to communicate to all that the project is over.

Begin the final report with a *high-level summary,* including the most significant results. In the remainder of the report, stress the accomplishments of the project team and formally recognize significant contributions made by individuals and groups to the project. Include **project retrospective metrics** and other performance information.

Add the final project report to the *project information archive,* along with any other project documents and reports that are updated or created as part of your project close-out.

Contracts and Accounting

Complete all paperwork required for contracted services used on the project and approve appropriate final payments. If there are issues or problems relating to a contract, escalate and resolve them as soon as possible. Complete

contract close-out following payment of all invoices, taking action to *terminate the contract.*

Summarize required financial information for the project and ensure that any *project accounting* is done accurately and promptly.

Thank Team Members

At the end of a project, *thank people,* both in person and in writing. For contributors who report to others, acknowledge their work formally to their managers. Use **rewards and recognition** as positive reinforcements for deserving project contributors.

Celebration

Celebrate success at the end of a project with an event. Even if the project had problems, identify accomplishments and do something to end the project on a positive note. Celebrations need not be lavish to be effective. On **global teams,** arrange similar events for each location.

Project Retrospective Analysis

At the end of a project, conduct a *post-project analysis* to capture **lessons learned.** Meet with the project team soon after the completion of project work to list practices that went well and should be used on future projects. Also identify project processes that need change, and generate recommendations for remedy. Document the results and add the report to the project information archive.

5 **Brainstorming**

WHAT: Using a team to generate many ideas.

WHEN: Throughout a project.

RESULTS: A large number of options for consideration.

Prepare

Brainstorming is useful for *generating alternatives* in many situations, such as

➤ project plan development

➤ risk response planning

➤ scope definition, cause-and-effect analysis

➤ decision making

➤ creative problem solving

Brainstorming is a *group technique,* depending on **teamwork** and interaction for good results. Gather people who can be expected to have insight into the current situation or problem to develop ideas.

Clearly present the *problem statement,* and encourage discussion if it is unclear. Post the statement where it will be visible to everyone.

Generate Ideas

Begin the process by providing paper or yellow sticky notes to the team members and encouraging them to write down as many ideas as they are able *on their own,* in silence. Capture each idea on a separate piece of paper. Minimize distractions, and request that people who finish first remain quiet while others continue to work.

When everyone is done, ask each person to read one of his or her ideas aloud and post each idea where it is visible to the group. When you have heard from everyone, continue until you have accumulated all the ideas in a *single list.* Include any new ideas that people generate while listening to other's submissions.

When gathering the ideas, allow *no discussions,* criticism, or questions. Focus on collecting the inputs as quickly as possible.

When the team can see all the ideas, ask if anyone has any *questions* about the items on the list. Allow the person who contributed the idea to answer questions initially, but encourage other participants to help refine the wording. Before making significant changes, get agreement from the person who generated the idea.

Organize the List

When there are no more questions, *condense the list.* If some ideas are similar, work to combine them into one. If ideas seem similar, but the people who contributed them think they are different, leave them listed separately.

Truncate the list, if necessary. If the list is longer than twenty items, give everyone three or four votes to indicate favored ideas, and reduce the list by selecting the ideas with the most support.

Prioritize the remaining ideas using a systematic process. You could discuss ideas further to generate information on costs and benefits, or apply systematic **decision making** using weighted criteria and relative evaluations. Another method is to have each person rank order the ideas on the list and use the rankings to define an overall team prioritization.

As a team, *consider the best option* and discuss any issues or potential problems associated with it. If no one has any objections, bring the brainstorming session to a close. If members disagree, consider the next two or three items on the list, or revise your evaluation method. Strive for a consensus that all can support.

Document the result and *put it to use.*

6 Canceling Projects

WHAT: Terminating a troubled project before its scheduled completion.

WHEN: Project execution and control.

RESULTS: Minimized time, effort, and money expended on doomed projects, and improved long-term team motivation.

Not every project, no matter how worthy or promising, will end well. When it becomes apparent that a project *will not ultimately succeed*, canceling it early, in a positive way, has many benefits.

Recognize the Situation

One reason for early termination is *insufficient progress* toward the **project objective. Performance reporting** may reveal:

➤ Schedule delays or execution problems

➤ Funding or resource consumption too high

➤ Insufficient staff or other resources

➤ Scope not achievable using available technologies and capabilities

Other reasons for ending projects relate to higher-level *business considerations,* such as:

➤ Changes in overall business strategy

➤ Shifts of priority to more urgent project or non-project work

➤ Recognition that too many simultaneous projects are underway

➤ Loss of funding or sponsorship

Assess the Situation

Perform a **project review** and validate your **plan variance analysis.** Use **cause-and-effect analysis** to understand the sources of project problems. *Explore options* for continuing, such as **negotiating project changes,** renewing **sponsorship of the project, problem escalation,** or other alternatives.

Terminate

If the project cannot be rescued, document the situation and *communicate* it to all stakeholders. Include a summary of the status, along with any alternatives you considered, and your recommendations for the timing and staffing of project closure. If appropriate, document the requirements for possible later resumption of the project.

Get approval for cancellation, and bring the work to a *logical conclusion*. Complete **administrative closure:**

➤ Document the results that have been achieved.

➤ Capture **lessons learned** and clearly describe the situation that resulted in early termination.

➤ Archive the project data in your project management information system.

➤ Acknowledge contributions.

➤ Close out project contracts and complete any financial requirements.

Bring the project to as positive a conclusion as possible. Work to let everyone involved *move on* from the project to other work with enthusiasm. Discourage "bridge burning" and "blame-storming."

7 Cause-and-Effect Analysis

WHAT: Determining the sources of a problem situation.

WHEN: Throughout a project.

RESULTS: Root causes for identified current or potential project trouble.

Sources of Trouble

Cause-and-effect analysis is applied in a wide range of situations, such as:

➤ **Risk response planning**

➤ **Process improvement**

➤ Problem solving

➤ **Schedule control**

➤ **Cost control**

➤ **Scope change control**

➤ Failure diagnosis

There are many names for essentially *similar processes,* including root cause analysis, failure mode and effect analysis, "fishbone diagrams," and Ishikawa charts, named for Dr. Kaoru Ishikawa, the Japanese quality movement expert who popularized the concepts.

Describe the Effect

Whatever the process is called, it begins with a clear, *unambiguous statement* of the problem, issue, risk, or other adverse situation. Quantify the effect, defining the consequences in terms that are as specific and measurable as possible.

Involve project *team members* and stakeholders with insight into the effect. Ensure that each person understands the situation and can describe it in his or her own words.

Identify Root Causes

As a group, **brainstorm** possible sources for the undesirable outcome. Collect as many inputs from the team as quickly as you can. Tap sources of data such as documented problems, **lessons learned** and other documentation from prior projects, checklists, and templates. Use the idea from **quality planning** of "asking why five times" to probe for causes, not symptoms. Focus on the quantity of ideas, not the quality; you can filter later.

Organize the results into major *cause categories* such as:

➤ Scope

➤ Schedule

➤ Staff

➤ Resources

➤ Organization

Diagram and Document

Display root causes visually, using a *fishbone diagram* to provide deeper understanding of the situation. Use subcategories as needed to organize the information logically, and review the results to see whether they stimulate additional causes.

Document the root causes and apply them to resolve the problem situation.

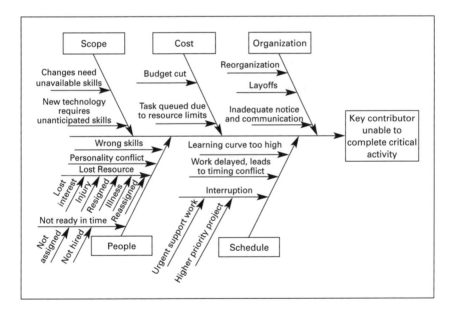

8 Coaching and Mentoring

WHAT: Sharing expertise with team members and building needed skills.

WHEN: Throughout a project.

RESULTS: Improved teamwork and better project performance.

Seek Opportunities to Help

Identify *capability gaps* in the project using **required skills analysis.** Identify proficiencies the project needs or would benefit from that are missing or insufficient. Use coaching for **performance problem resolution.**

Assess weaknesses on the project team and consider *threats and risks* that could require responses using specialized talents.

Align *personal goals* with project and organizational needs. Ask team members what they desire to learn and do, and use the information to guide **team development** and increase **motivation.** Keep the "big picture" and **project vision** in sight, and identify opportunities to develop new skills on the project team when **delegating responsibility.**

Foster an Open Environment

Build *trust* and **teamwork,** so people will feel free to discuss any matter or topic without fear of criticism. Encourage "pull"; respond positively to requests for help and encourage project staff members to let you know when they are inexperienced or lack skills needed for their assigned activities. Display **leadership;** model the behaviors you wish to see on the project: follow through on commitments, make time for **communicating informally,** and be willing to teach and share your expertise.

Confidentiality

Effective mentoring requires *discretion.* People need to feel free to reveal their shortcomings and ask "dumb questions." Since this may not be the case when the mentor is also the individual's manager, mentoring is generally most successful across organizational boundaries, where there will not be repercussions or consequences.

Ongoing Relationships

Build on coaching and mentoring relationships over time. Establish *long-term* two-way relationships, where in some cases the roles reverse, and the mentor requests guidance. Encourage people who benefit from mentoring to share what they have learned with others by becoming mentors.

9 Communicating Informally

WHAT: Periodic person-to-person communication without a specific purpose.

WHEN: Throughout a project.

RESULTS: Good team relationships, fewer misunderstandings, and early warning of potential problems.

Informal communication is often as (or more) important on projects as formal communication. Many risks and problems surface first through conversations and other team interactions, and **teamwork** and relationship building depend upon it.

Unstructured

Some of the most important project communication takes place through casual *conversations* at coffee machines, in corridors, and parking lots. Successful project leaders make an effort to encourage frequent, unstructured conversations, both with and between team members. "Soft data" and valuable project information often surfaces during unplanned exchanges.

Even with **global teams,** where you are seldom able to talk with people in person, there may be opportunities to do it once in a while; always take full advantage of face-to-face opportunities to enhance relationships. Use the *telephone* when you are at a distance. Call team members regularly, even when there may be no pressing project business, to ask how they are doing.

Structured

Many project leaders set aside time at least once a week to "*manage by wandering around.*" MBWA is a particularly effective way to reinforce trust and build relationships within a project team. While it is best done in person and with no particular objective, it can also be a part of regularly scheduled one-on-one meetings or telephone calls for **status collection** or discussion of **delegated responsibilities.** Asking questions about interests, family matters, or other non-project matters adds a personal touch and helps build **motivation,** particularly if you keep it brief and restrict yourself to topics both of you are interested in discussing.

Informal communications are also an important benefit of *team activities,* longer meetings (such as **start-up workshops** and **project reviews**), and project celebrations. Use milestones and other key project dates to organize events that are at least partly social, to reinforce the connections on the team. Particularly for longer projects, "extracurricular" activities are effective in maintaining teamwork, but let the team choose the event. Avoid "forced merriment" and diversions that may annoy or distract the team. Eating together, scheduling an outing to a film, or engaging in some other event of mutual interest builds team cohesion essential to a healthy project.

10 Communications Planning (PMBOK® 10.1)

WHAT: Documenting communications decisions for a project.

WHEN: Project planning.

RESULTS: A communications infrastructure that ensures timely and effective communication and supports smooth project execution.

Determine Communication Requirements

Review the **project infrastructure** decisions, and determine how all formal communications will be done. Define the internal reporting required for the project team and external communication for sponsor, stakeholders, and others. Assign responsibility for all project communications, and schedule routine communications to support **project plan execution**.

If the project involves *confidential* or proprietary information, document how it will be handled.

Determine how project communications will be done. Plan to take advantage of all **information distribution** and *communications methods* available. Throughout the project use all types of communications: formal and informal, written and verbal.

Develop a plan for *archiving project data* and communications in a project management information system (often referred to as a PMIS), including project definition documents, project plans, status reports and presentations, logs of project issues and approved changes, and project closure reports. If data will be stored online, determine what you may need to do to permit or restrict access.

Document the Plan and Get Approval

Record your decisions and identify anything in the communications plan that requires hardware you do not possess or will generate expenses beyond what is expected for the project. Present your plan to your sponsor for review and get approval for it.

Implement Your Plan

Install any teleconferencing equipment or other hardware necessary to communicate with distant **virtual team** members, and test systems before their first scheduled use. If there are problems, schedule any upgrades or maintenance promptly and coordinate any planned changes to ensure ongoing compatibility.

11 Conflict Resolution

WHAT: Gaining team agreement following a difference of opinion.

WHEN: Throughout a project.

RESULTS: Ongoing cooperation and team cohesion.

Conflict Sources

Whenever people work together, there is potential for conflict. Avoiding disagreements begins with *minimizing causes.* Typical problems and remedies include:

Causes of conflict	Avoidance tactics
Overlapping responsibility	➤ Clear **activity definition** ➤ Unambiguously outlining each person's role
Differing cultures, viewpoints, perspectives, and backgrounds	➤ Building **teamwork** ➤ Conducting a project **start-up workshop** ➤ Avoiding unnecessary interactions that depend on **global team working styles**
Misunderstandings	➤ Thorough **communications planning** ➤ Effective **information distribution**
Lack of trust and relationships	➤ Periodic face-to-face **meetings**

Overall Methods

Detect conflicts early and deal with problems while they are still small. *Probe for information* using open-ended questions, seeking to understand the source of the disagreement.

Conflict management modes include forcing (imposing unity through authority), withdrawing (moving on to other work without resolution), smoothing (minimizing conflict by improving interpersonal relationships), confrontation, and compromise. For teams that must work together throughout a project, only the last two are effective in the long term. Sometimes it is not possible to resolve conflicts in ways that everyone prefers, so successful resolution often involves seeking a "third way," different from the initial ideas held by team members but acceptable to all.

Face the Issues

Resolving internal team conflicts begins with *meeting in person* (or via suitable conferencing techniques) so people can discuss matters openly.

Clearly state the problem situation, and verify that everyone *wants to resolve* the conflict.

Consider All Perspectives

Allow each person to *present his or her perspective* on the issue, without allowing any comments or criticism from others.

Clarifying questions are permitted, but narrowly *focus on facts and data,* not on personality and emotion. Using active listening, paraphrasing, constructive feedback, and open questions.

Quantify the alternatives and options discussed in terms of time, money, or other specific units that will support objective comparisons.

Seek "Win–Win" Resolutions

Brainstorm other alternatives and *combinations of ideas* presented. Use the information you have to develop new, better ideas with potentially broader acceptance.

Use systematic **decision making** to reach *common agreement,* or at least a resolution that everyone will accept.

Confirm closure and document what was decided.

If You Find No Resolution

In the case of especially significant external barriers and internal conflicts, you may fail to resolve the situation within your team. **Problem escalation** should always be a last resort, but a *forcing solution,* imposed by the project sponsor or others with more authority, may be necessary occasionally. Use this tactic sparingly; frequent escalations can lead to team resentment, malicious compliance, and future project conflict.

12 Consensus Building for Your Ideas

WHAT: Creating team support for your ideas.

WHEN: Throughout a project.

RESULTS: Group buy-in and agreement for your plan of action.

Note: This process is suitable for project situations where you need to gain approval from a group to implement an idea. For general group problem solving, use the **decision-making** process.

Plan

Outline the situation requiring your response. After documenting it, write down any alternatives that you have for dealing with it. Do not limit yourself to considering only the option you prefer.

Identify all the team members, *stakeholders,* and others from whom you must obtain buy-in.

From the perspectives of these decision makers, *analyze* each possible response, noting the benefits, costs, and any possible objections. If your preferred response remains the best overall alternative, develop credible answers for any objections you can anticipate.

Document your analysis, outlining the situation, your proposed response, and clearly specified and quantified benefits and costs. If you expect to have to do a formal **presentation,** organize it carefully, and rehearse what you plan to say.

Meet

Schedule a time and place to meet with the people who need to agree on your proposal. Get their commitment to attend.

Set an *agenda* for the **meeting** that covers presentation and discussion of the problem situation, analysis by the group, and closure with a decision.

Discuss the details of the situation, and the consequences of taking no action.

Present a summary of your proposed response, emphasizing its *main benefits.* Continue discussing the details and show how your idea directly addresses the needs.

Invite questions, criticism, concerns, and objections. Acknowledge them and *respond* to them using the information you prepared. Encourage people to propose modifications to your proposal that might improve it, and adopt any beneficial suggestions.

Ask if anyone has an *alternative* course of action that he or she would like to present. If there are any, discuss them along with yours. Use the information on alternatives you developed before the meeting to raise any issues concerning costs or other deficiencies.

Summarize the *merits* of your proposal and of any alternative ideas discussed. Focus the summary on areas of agreement within the group.

Seek *consensus* from the group for a single idea. If your preparation was thorough and your proposal has merit, the group will choose your idea.

Acknowledge the agreement, *document* the decision, and close the meeting.

Take Action

Communicate the decision to all project contributors, and *implement* your idea.

13 Constraint Management and Plan Optimization

WHAT: Resolving differences between project constraints and your bottom-up plans.

WHEN: Project planning, execution, and control.

RESULTS: A project schedule that is consistent with top-down objectives, or the best option and several alternatives.

Document Constraints and Limitations

Toward the conclusion of **project plan development,** *review and document* the **project objective,** assumptions, and constraints identified at **project initiation.** Note also:

➤ Intermediate milestones and key *target dates*

➤ Profiles of *available staffing* effort from **resource planning**

➤ Technical and other **required skills analysis,** with any *skill gaps* uncovered in **responsibility analysis**

➤ *Interfaces* and dependencies linking to any **multiple dependent projects**

➤ Any *other limitations* or issues identified in the planning process

Identify Discrepancies Between the Bottom-Up Plans and Goals

Compare stated project goals with your plans. Determine any issues between your **schedule development** and the project deadline. Identify differences between the project budget derived from **cost estimation** and the budget limits for the project. Outline any scope issues between defined project deliverables and what your project team is realistically capable of producing.

Document any significant *additional differences* between timing and specification of interim deliverables, the profiles from **resource leveling,** unavailable skills, or any other variances between your plan and project requirements.

Use Priorities to Explore Trade-offs

Review **project priorities,** and use **brainstorming** to develop *plan modifications* consistent with them. If schedule is the top priority, modify resources and scope as necessary to align project completion with the defined project deadline. **Software tools for project management** can make "what if?" exploration of project options easier.

Possible resource plan changes include:

➤ Locating and rescheduling work to use *resource undercommitments*

➤ *Delaying noncritical work*

➤ *Moving staff to more critical work* from noncritical activities

➤ *Outsourcing or adding staff* from other parts of the organization

➤ *Upgrading or replacing equipment* to improve efficiency

➤ *Increasing performance* through **process improvement**

➤ *Automating manual work*

➤ Using **rewards and recognition** to *improve productivity* and **motivation**

➤ *Building new skills* through training or **coaching and mentoring**

➤ *Decreasing interruptions,* distractions, and other commitments

Frequently there are project specifications that are not essential or not time critical. Consider modifications to project scope, such as:

➤ Prioritizing specifications and *deleting less important features*

➤ *Delaying some requirements* to a follow-on project

➤ *Phasing the delivery of results* over a longer timeframe

➤ *Reducing complexity* of the required work

➤ *Finding opportunities for reuse and leverage*

➤ *Buying needed components* instead of making them

Even if timing is your highest priority, consider changes to the schedule:

➤ *Revising activity dependencies*

➤ *Using float to accelerate critical tasks,* delaying less critical work

➤ *Fast-tracking*—breaking activities into pieces executed in parallel

➤ *Starting work earlier* than currently scheduled

➤ *"Crashing"* work by adding resources

➤ *Scheduling work on non-workdays* (but this can backfire)

Document the Plan(s)

Consider changes you are empowered to make, and strive to develop a plan to *meet your project objective* and constraints. If you are successful, gain support from the team, document the resulting plan, and use it for **project base-line setting.**

If your best efforts still *fall short of the project objective,* document at least two plan alternatives that come as close as possible and at least meet the primary project priority. These alternative plans provide the data you need to **negotiate project changes** with your sponsor and stakeholders before committing to a baseline for **project plan execution.**

14 Contract Administration (PMBOK® 12.5)

WHAT: Managing outsourced work and supplier relationships, based on an existing contract.

WHEN: Project execution and control.

RESULTS: Open, two-way communication, appropriate and timely deliverables, management of changes, and payment for services.

Managing the Relationship

Make one project team member responsible for each supplier relationship. This person's initial *liaison* duty is to discuss the contract thoroughly with the assigned primary contact for the other party to ensure that everyone understands the contract terms. In addition, he or she will be responsible for routine communications, managing any changes, contract and payment matters, issue and problem management, and problem escalation.

Periodically, especially following any changes to the contract or staffing, *review* the terms and conditions in the contract.

Work to build **motivation** on the staff for outsourced work. Recognize people by thanking them for their efforts and praise good results. Strive to assign work required to *individuals who care* about it, and make ownership of tasks explicit.

Communicate

Collect status on outsourced work at least once per week, in writing. Find ways to *verify progress*; participate in inspections, walk-throughs, interim tests, and other reviews. Schedule well-defined milestones with deliverables frequently in subcontracted work, especially with new suppliers. Make outsourced work as visible as possible. Maintain a record of all formal communication with suppliers in your project archives.

In addition to status communication, schedule a *general discussion* meeting with suppliers at least once a month, face-to-face if possible. **Communicating informally** is also necessary; keep the channels of communications open, and work to maintain trust and a good, honest working relationship. When there are problems, focus on recovery and problem solving, not on fixing blame.

Measurement and Payment

Evaluate all interim and final deliverables using criteria consistent with the terms of the contract and the statement of work finalized during **source selection**. Include contracted work in your project **performance reporting**.

Note any *deviations* from the contract requirements, such as timing, accuracy, or quality. Work with the supplier to resolve them, or at least minimize their impact on the project. If resolution proves beyond your control, promptly move to **problem escalation**.

Ensure that all *payments* called for in the contract are made based on successful achievement of project milestones and satisfactory acceptance criteria. If payments are reduced because of performance or other issues, document the situation in writing, and support any deductions by including relevant contract terms in your communications to the supplier.

Changes

Manage all changes using the *documented process* in the contract and be consistent with your **integrated change control** process. Contract changes are often expensive and have other undesirable consequences, so avoid them whenever possible. If a necessary change goes beyond the terms of the contract or exceeds its financial limits, amend the contract and have both parties re-sign it, or negotiate a new contract to replace the original one.

15 Contract Closeout (PMBOK® 12.6)

WHAT: Verifying successful performance at the conclusion of outsourced work, completion of documentation, and closure of the contract.

WHEN: Project execution or closure.

RESULTS: Receipt of all contract deliverables, final payments, and termination of the contract.

Verify Completion

At the completion of contracted work, compare the results achieved with the contract requirements (and any approved changes). Validate satisfactory achievement of each *specified requirement.*

Work with the supplier to resolve any *remaining variances,* successfully completing all needed work. If some portions of the work cannot be completed, determine the consequences in terms or payments, penalties, or other actions.

If early *contract termination* becomes necessary, because of **canceling projects** or other circumstances, this should be done using the terms set out in the contract. Document all the work that was completed, and determine the financial and other consequences of early termination.

Final Payment

Review the contract terms and the contract payment history. Approve prompt payment of the *final invoice,* consistent with the financial obligations remaining on the contract.

Documentation

Evaluate the performance of the supplier and document the **lessons learned** as part of your **administrative closure** for your project information archive. Be particularly thorough if the contracted work ends substantially before the end of the project.

File all contract communication, accounting reports, status and other project reports, change history, and other relevant *documents* for reference on your future projects and for use by your peers responsible for similar project work.

16 **Cost Budgeting** (PMBOK ® 7.3)

WHAT: Determining the overall expected project cost, based on bottom-up planning.

WHEN: Project planning, execution, and control.

RESULTS: A realistic budget for the project derived from detailed planning data.

Identify Direct Project Costs

Project **cost estimation** at the activity level, central to **project plan development,** provides the basis of cost budgeting. List all activity-related expenses for:

➤ *Staffing costs* (based on effort estimates and appropriate labor rates)

➤ *Outsourcing* (from **source selection** and **negotiating contracts**)

➤ *Hardware* and other equipment purchases

➤ Charges for use of *shared or rented equipment*

➤ *Supplies* and required components

➤ *Software* acquisition and licenses

➤ *Communications:* audio, video, computer networking

➤ *Services*: shipping costs, duplicating, and printing

➤ *Travel expenses*

➤ *Other needs* with direct costs

Determine the Project Budget and Project Cost Profile

Cost budgeting begins by accumulating these costs for the entire project. The *overall project budget* is the sum of all of the bottom-up costs associated with project activities plus any project-level expenses for **staff acquisition,** overhead, or other indirect costs allocated to the project. For longer projects, you may also need to consider factors such as salary changes and the effects of inflation.

The project budget also includes *budget reserve,* if any was established for the project during **risk response planning.** The total of all these costs forecasts the project budget at completion (BAC)

Project budget data can also be combined with **schedule development** to create a *cost profile* for the project. You can generate resource histograms for overall project costs using spreadsheets, project databases, and other methods, for the project as a whole or for specific cost categories. This same analysis process is applied to **resource leveling.** The overall project cost profile also provides much of the information used for **return on investment analysis.**

Profiles and histograms of costs (or effort) associated with staffing may be generated using **software tools for project management.** This is the foundation of *planned value* (or budgeted cost of work scheduled, BCWS), used for **earned value management.** This period-by-period cost information displays when the project is expected to require various levels of effort. Earned value analysis may be done using either effort statistics or overall costs.

Review Project Costs

Contrast the overall project budget with the project objective to determine whether the bottom-up analysis is consistent with the initial expectations of the project sponsor and stakeholders. If there are significant variances, either with the overall costs or with the timing of the costs, *minimize the differences* through **constraint management and plan optimization.**

If problems still remain after your best replanning efforts, *resolve budget issues* by **negotiating project changes.**

Manage the Project Budget

Document the project cost baseline and use it to track project performance during **project plan execution.**

Develop a project *budget management plan* and periodically revise it as necessary during **project reviews.**

17 **Cost Control** (PMBOK® 7.4)

WHAT: Monitoring project costs and managing use of project resources.

WHEN: Project execution and control.

RESULTS: A record of project costs, with plan adjustments as required to meet budget expectations.

Determine Status and Analyze Variances

Cost control is central to **project plan execution.** It follows **status collection** and **plan variance analysis** in the project tracking cycle. It is necessary in any cycle where you discover a significant cost or effort variance, or your **earned value management** measurements are out of limit. For each variance, review its *root cause and impact* on the project timeline. Determine whether the impact is a one-time or short-term issue, or whether the root cause is a longer term—a chronic problem or part of an adverse trend.

Plan Responses

Review your **project infrastructure** decisions and **integrated change control** process to *ensure consistency* with agreed-upon principles.

Involve the project *team members* in your planning; engage as many perspectives and points of view as practical.

Depending on the severity of the problem and the nature of its root cause, the *type of response* may be:

➤ A minor change that preserves the **project objective**

➤ Implementation of a contingency plan developed during **risk response planning**

➤ A major change to the project

For *short-term* effort problems, consider "brute force" solutions, such as working overtime in the evenings or on nonworkdays.

For more significant problems, **brainstorm** approaches that could resolve the resource variance. Explore options using the processes of **project plan development,** especially **constraint management and plan optimization.** Develop plans that deal with the root cause of the problem, not just the symptoms. Avoid adopting the first alternative you develop; work to generate *several credible responses.* Typical responses include:

➤ **Resource leveling**

➤ Lengthening the schedule

➤ Finding lower-cost alternatives for project work

➤ Borrowing resources from other projects

➤ Reducing the scope of the project deliverable

➤ Responses that were effective in similar past situations

For problems that cannot be solved using conventional analysis, use **creative problem solving.** Allocate a reasonable amount of time to plan a response, but avoid "analysis paralysis." Set a time limit for planning and use systematic **decision making** to choose the *best idea* available within that limit.

Take Action and Document Results

Validate the response you select before you implement it. Verify that your proposal is consistent with your **project priorities.** If the response involves changes to the deliverable, get approval for it through **scope change control.** Discuss any major changes with the project sponsor and appropriate stakeholders. If necessary, use **problem escalation** to obtain approval. Very major changes may result in new **project baseline setting.**

Inform the project team and appropriate stakeholders of your plans and *implement the response.*

Following your implementation, monitor to ensure that your response obtained the *expected results* and did not lead to adverse unforeseen consequences. If problems persist, seek a better solution though additional planning.

Update any project and *planning documents* that are affected by the actions, and reflect any new estimates in your **project budgeting.** Communicate the results of your efforts in project **performance reporting.**

18 **Cost Estimating** (PMBOK® 7.2)

WHAT: Forecasting the costs of project activities.

WHEN: Project planning, execution, and control.

RESULTS: Resource cost estimates for all defined project activities.

Determine Effort

Cost and effort estimates are a central component of **project plan development.** For each listed task in your project **activity definition,** use **resource planning** data to develop *effort estimates,* in units combining staffing and time, such as person-days or engineer-hours. Useful sources to assist with estimating include:

➤ *History* (**lessons learned,** databases of **project diagnostic metrics,** information from **earned value management**)

➤ *Activity owner analysis* and personal experience

➤ *Analogs* (previous work of a similar type)

➤ *Experts* (consultants, peers, managers, vendor proposals)

➤ *Published data* (WWW, papers, articles, professional magazines)

➤ *Parametric, or size-based formulas* ("rules of thumb," complexity analysis, component or module counts, function points and other code assessments, measurements of volume, area, length, or other parameters)

➤ *Team analysis* (**Delphi technique,** further work decomposition)

Refine Effort Estimates and Reconcile with Duration Estimates

Adjust effort estimates for your specific project. Consider resource and staffing factors such as:

➤ Project *constraints and assumptions*

➤ **Required skills analysis** and *staff capabilities*

➤ *Staff availability*

➤ *Staff productivity*

➤ Activities that are *not fully staffed* by named, committed contributors

➤ *Delays* in **staff acquisition**

➤ *Potential turnover*

- ➤ The project *work environment* and frequency of interruptions
- ➤ *Team size*
- ➤ *Communications* and **meetings**
- ➤ *Geographical separation* of team members
- ➤ Conflicting **project priorities** with *other work*
- ➤ *Training* and learning curve issues

Effort estimation and **activity duration estimation** are closely linked. Which you do first for project planning does not matter much, but *ensure consistency* before finalizing a baseline plan.

Determine the normal number of *work hours available* in a workday for project activities after removing meetings, e-mail, telephone calls, breaks, meals, and other interruptions. Five to six hours may be available, but for some contributors the total is lower.

Adjust duration estimates to make them consistent with your effort analysis, or determine how to **negotiate project changes** to obtain resources to support them.

Calculate Costs and Adjust for Uncertainty

Convert effort estimates into monetary costs using appropriate *labor rates.*

For each project activity, determine *other expenses,* for outsourcing, equipment, software, travel, support, training, communication, and other direct activity costs. Sum the labor and other costs to determine a "most likely" activity cost estimate.

Once you have made a "most likely" cost estimate, probe for failure modes and potential problems. Determine the cost and resource consequences of *worst cases.*

PERT (Program Evaluation and Review Technique) defines a formula you may use to adjust cost estimates for uncertainty: $c_e = (c_o + 4c_m + c_p)/6$, where c_e is a weighted average "expected" cost, based on c_o: an optimistic cost, c_m: the most likely cost, and c_p: a pessimistic cost.

Capture Cost Data

Document costs for project work to support **cost budgeting** and **resource leveling** analysis. Associate costs by account or category if this is standard practice for your projects.

Revise cost and effort estimates as needed to resolve resource problems during the project through **cost control.**

Revalidate estimates periodically during **project reviews,** particularly for lengthy projects.

19 Creative Problem Solving

WHAT: Using novel or unconventional approaches to resolve project problems.

WHEN: Throughout a project.

RESULTS: Solutions to problems and situations that do not yield to "normal" techniques.

Problem

Novel approaches to problem solving may be necessary in many project situations, including:

➤ Decision making

➤ Project plan development

➤ Scope planning

➤ Conflict resolution

➤ Process improvement

➤ Risk response planning

Clearly *describe the problem* you face, in writing. Outline conventional approaches that you have applied to the problem and summarize why these methods failed to resolve the problem.

People

Work with a *diverse group* of others to stimulate thinking. Seek the help of people who have a track record of working creatively. Find help outside your normal work group—experts, people from other functions and disciplines, contributors with different backgrounds, cultures, and perspectives. Involve generalists with a wide range of knowledge, and mix beginners and experienced team members together. Strive for synergy in the team, where the sum of talent exceeds the capabilities of the individuals.

Environment

Creativity is less likely in familiar surroundings. Find a *novel place* to work—off site, outside, in someone else's workplace. Getting away from your normal work space also minimizes interruptions.

Provide an atmosphere where people can *take risks* without criticism. Foster a willingness to test new ideas and alternatives, and encourage the free cascading of thoughts. Encourage humor, fun, and positive interaction.

The best solutions may not emerge quickly; get commitment for the *time and effort* the problem deserves, but do set a reasonable time limit.

Approaches

Begin by **brainstorming** possibilities for resolution. Encourage everyone to think like a novice, without preconceived notions of what will not work. Be organized and *have a plan* for proceeding—avoid "getting stuck." The following approaches may help:

➤ Research technologies and alternatives.

➤ Use analogies. Look for similarities in other fields.

➤ Combine ideas into new concepts.

➤ "Misuse" techniques, ideas, and tools.

➤ Focus on what you can make work and attempt to expand on it.

➤ Be persistent. Develop partial answers and work them into full solutions.

➤ Tolerate errors and failure; seek ways to address the defects or succeed with related methods.

Keep track of unsuccessful approaches; if something does not work, move on. Within the allotted time, select the best available option for dealing with the problem.

Implement and Communicate

Use the developed solution to *deal with the problem* situation.

Document your solution and *communicate* it to others responsible for similar project work. Also, capture information on any approaches you found deficient to avoid future blind alleys.

20 Customer Interviews

WHAT: Discussions with customers and users of project deliverables to determine requirements and needs.

WHEN: Project initiation and planning, with periodic review during execution.

RESULTS: Clear knowledge of the customer environment, needs, and trends.

Plan the Interview

Interviews are a technique for one-on-one **user needs assessment.** Some interviews are part of the interaction with specific individuals who are project stakeholders. Other interviews are more generic, as part of qualitative **market research.** Whatever the purpose, *plan* the interview(s), estimating the required time, skills, costs for travel, and other expenses. Determine how many interviews you will need to do; twenty to thirty interviews are typical for market research. Set up appointments with the individuals you need to meet with well in advance. Obtain and test a tape recorder to use during the interviews.

Define what you need to learn, and develop a *discussion guide* to use during interviews to ensure that you consistently probe for the information you need. Do a practice interview with one of your team members before your first customer session.

If you will be able to interview a customer only once, ensure that the *people involved* will be able to adequately discuss all the topics of interest. Never conduct an interview alone; have at least one other person to take notes. If you are not fluent in the language of your customer, arrange for an interpreter.

Conduct the Interview

Arrive slightly early, to ensure that you keep your appointment. Following introductions, briefly *discuss your objectives* and reconfirm the customer's agreement. Request permission to record the interview and set up the tape recorder. If recording is not permitted, have a colleague take very thorough notes.

Ask your questions, but spend most of your time listening. You are there to collect the voice of the customer. *Collect information* by watching what happens. Work to understand what the customer does.

When you are finished, *thank the customer,* and follow up afterward with written thanks and responses to any questions you were unable to answer during the interview.

Capture Results

Discuss what you learned immediately after the interview, and summarize your interview findings promptly, in a consistent format. Soon after your last interview, *document your overall analysis.*

Use the customer interview information to complete **scope planning** and conduct follow-up interviews to support **project reviews.**

21 Decision Making

WHAT: Using a systematic process to select one option among competing alternatives.

WHEN: Throughout a project.

RESULTS: Team buy-in for a decision that can be expected to deliver good results.

Define the Issue or Question

Good decision making begins with a clear, *unambiguous statement* of the question that needs to be answered. Avoid beginning to solve problems prematurely, before you understand the issues. Use **cause-and-effect analysis** to probe for the source of the problem, not just the symptoms. Decompose complex issues into a number of smaller, simpler ones.

Frame the issue by defining what results a decision must produce. Define measures that signify successful resolution, and limit your considerations to things that you can influence or control.

Determine Logistics and Procedure

Decision making requires **teamwork;** determine *who needs to participate* and get their commitment to participate. If one or more distant team members are to participate, select times for conference calls that are acceptable to them.

Get agreement from participants on the *decision process* you will use.

Objective decisions require *defined criteria,* such as cost, time, usefulness, completeness, or feasibility. Seek criteria that relate to your defined goal, and make them measurable. Prioritize the criteria by relative importance. Also identify any constraints such as time, resources, or required approvals.

Develop Options

Work with the team to **brainstorm** *options.* Generate as many as you can in the time available. **Creative problem solving** techniques and **cause-and-effect analysis** can help in developing a wide range of possibilities. Research the possibilities; investigate what others have done through networking, browsing the WWW, and benchmarking.

Analyze Options and Decide

Filter the options generated through a quick assessment using your decision criteria, especially if you have generated a large number of alternatives. Restrict detailed analysis to no more than about six options.

Analyze the best options, determining estimates for each that relate to your decision criteria. When it is difficult to quantify the assessment, compare options in pairs to determine which alternatives are preferred by the team, and how strongly they are preferred. **Software tools for project management** may be useful in complex situations.

Use the assessments to *sequence the options,* and then discuss how people feel about the prioritized list. Test the top option with scenarios, models, or simulations, and think about possible unintended consequences and risks. If there are valid problems with the first option, consider the next alternative, or revise your decision criteria.

Use systematic analysis to *reach closure,* and document the decision made by the team.

Communicate and Implement the Decision

Document and *clearly communicate* the decision to all people affected by it.

Implement the decision and measure the results.

Be prepared to *revisit and adjust* decisions if they fail to deliver expected results. It is usually better to make decisions quickly, following up with necessary modifications, than to wait indefinitely for complete information.

22 Delegating Responsibility

WHAT: Setting individual goals and tracking them to completion.

WHEN: Project planning and execution.

RESULTS: Commitment by team members to goals that align with business and project objectives.

Set Goals

When setting goals, both the project leader and the individual team member involved should *create lists* of work to be accomplished. The lists should include, but not be limited to, items from **activity definition** where the individual is an owner or participant. Strive to capture all significant current responsibilities. Schedule a meeting time to discuss goals.

Make one list by combining the items from the leader's and the individual's lists. For any goal that appears only on one list, discuss it and agree that it is valid before adding it. If there are similar goals on the two lists, develop a single, consensus description.

Test that each goal described on the list is:

➤ *SMART:* specific, measurable, assignable, realistic, time-bounded

➤ *Stable* (if it may change, list one or more shorter-term goals)

➤ *Aligned* with business and **project objectives**

➤ *Coherent* (all the goals listed make logical sense together)

➤ *Clear* (the intended result is unambiguous)

To enhance **motivation,** include at least one goal that relates to a *personal preference* or desire for development.

Outline the *benefits* of achieving the goals to the individual, the project, and the overall organization. Uncover potential problems with goals through **risk identification.** If needed, modify goals to reduce risk.

Review the *target date* for each goal. Validate the activity duration estimates and cost estimates for all project activities where the individual is the owner. Modify unrealistic dates, and reflect any changes made in project planning documents. Ensure that the highest priority goals are scheduled for completion as early as practical and discuss the consequences of late completion in specific, measurable terms.

Document all current goals on the list, including any details on costs, timing, staffing, and external dependencies.

Get commitment for the goals on the list and express your confidence in the individual's ability to complete them successfully. Schedule periodic follow-up meetings to review goals and discuss progress.

Review and Update Goals

Prior to the follow-up meeting, *prepare to review* progress on the list of goals. Assemble data from **status collection** and if necessary, prepare a list of potential new goals to replace those that have been completed.

Begin the meeting by discussing finished work and goals showing satisfactory progress. *Recognize good performance* and thank the contributor for any goals completed. Consider **rewards and recognition** for completion of significant accomplishments.

Use **plan variance analysis** to identify any *unmet goals* or any project work that is falling behind schedule. Use the follow-up meeting to confront each **performance problem,** and determine whether it is best to adjust the goal, replace it, or drop it.

Discuss any proposed *new goals* and add them to the current list of goals. Reprioritize the resulting list, and adjust the dates on the goals as necessary.

To end the meeting, *document the updated goals,* and confirm the place and time for your next progress review meeting.

For any goals that have slipped or have been changed, *communicate* new schedule information to any people or **multiple dependent projects** that may be affected.

Keep a *history* of goals and accomplishments for **project reviews,** evaluations, and analysis of **lessons learned.**

23 **Delphi Technique**

WHAT: Using group input to refine forecasts and estimates.

WHEN: Project planning, execution, and control.

RESULTS: Credible responses to questions requiring quantitative answers, even when supporting data is sparse.

Define the Question

Delphi technique draws on "group intelligence" and relies on the fact that although no one person may be able to provide reliable estimates confidently, the middle range of estimates drawn from a population of stakeholders is frequently a realistic predictor for numeric results. Delphi taps into *undocumented history,* often yielding very realistic estimates and forecasts. The collaborative process also builds **motivation,** ownership, buy-in, and **teamwork.**

To begin the process, clearly *state the question* requiring a numeric answer, such as:

➤ **Activity duration estimates**

➤ **Cost estimates**

➤ **Quantitative risk analysis** of impact or probability

➤ **Decision making**

➤ Forecasts for **return on investment analysis**

Gather *five or more people* who possess relevant experience and knowledge, even though they may not have confidence that they can answer with precision. **Meetings** in person are best, but **virtual team** meetings can be effective.

Provide data on the question: facts, issues, constraints, and assumptions. Share *information* on any aspect except for your opinion on the answer.

Familiarize the team on the *Delphi process* if it is new to them.

Collect Responses

From each individual, collect a response to the question. The responses should be given quickly and *without any consultation.* Responses can be either anonymous or attributed.

Sort responses into three roughly equal groups: Highest, Middle, and Lowest.

Discuss the Outcome

After collecting the individual responses, encourage *group discussion.* Explore:

➤ Are the most pessimistic responses based on specific experiences?

➤ Are there credible shortcuts or innovative methods that support the optimistic responses?

➤ Is the average of the middle responses reasonable?

Repeat the Process

Collect *another set* of individual responses. After collection, group and discuss them.

Convergence in two to three cycles is common for most project-related questions. Strive for *consensus,* or at least an answer that all on the team will accept.

Document and use the outcome of the Delphi process.

24 Earned Value Management (EVM)

WHAT: Using predictive and diagnostic project metrics to determine project performance.

WHEN: Project planning, execution, and control.

RESULTS: Early detection of resource overconsumption issues, and reliable forecasts of adverse budget and schedule trends.

Basis

Earned value management (EVM) seems complex, but it has a simple foundation. **Project plan development** generates a schedule and a budget. **Project plan execution** generates real data, resulting in an actual schedule and an actual budget. EVM is one way to assess the *differences* between these schedules and budgets. EVM evaluates project progress in terms of **project diagnostic metrics** (using resource units, either money or effort) related to these schedules and budgets in various combinations. The three principal metrics for EVM are:

		Budgets	
		Planned Expenses	Actual Expenses
Schedules	Planned Schedule	Planned Value (BCWS)	
	Actual Schedule	Earned Value (BCWP)	Actual Cost (ACWP)

(There is no EVM metric combining the baseline schedule with actual expense.) EVM tracks planned and actual cumulative resource consumption at the level of project activities. When all three of these metrics are the same, a project is considered on time and on budget.

The first requirement for EVM is **cost estimating** for each activity, allocating the entire project budget to the planned project activities. The sum of all these allocations must equal exactly 100 percent of the project budget. *Planned value* (PV), also called the budgeted cost of work scheduled (BCWS), is a running accumulation of these costs for the entire project based on the project schedule. Because PV may be calculated from the baseline plan, it is actually a **project predictive metric,** but for EVM it is generally treated as a diagnostic metric, calculated periodically along with the other measures.

Where PV is based on the planned schedule and planned budget, *actual cost* (AC) is calculated using the actual schedule and budget. AC, sometimes referred to as the actual cost of work performed (ACWP), is a running accumulation of the actual costs for every project activity that is currently complete. EVM does not directly compare PV and AC because their differences may result from budget issues, schedule variances, or both.

To untangle the comparison problem, *earned value* (EV) is derived from a combination of the planned budget and the actual schedule. EV, defined as the budgeted cost of work performed (BCWP), is the running accumulation of the costs that were planned for every project activity currently complete.

Analysis

Actual costs are assessed throughout the project through **status collection.** For a given date, EV and PV are most commonly calculated using the "50/50" rule—accumulating half the planned cost on the start date and the other half at the finish. EVM metrics may also use interpolated estimates for **performance reporting.**

Budget performance is assessed by combining earned value and actual cost. These metrics are both based on the actual schedule, so any difference must result from resource consumption. The *cost performance* (CP) is EV minus AC, a quantitative measure of how much the project is currently over (or under) budget. The ratio of EV and AC is the *cost performance index* (CPI),

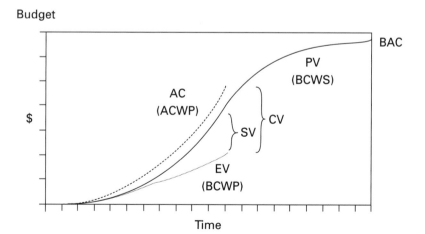

revealing the state of the project budget as a percentage. Positive CP, or a CPI above one, indicates a project that is under budget.

Schedule performance is assessed by combining earned value and planned value. Both EV and PV are based on the planned budget, so any difference in the two must result from schedule variance. *Schedule performance* (SP) is EV minus PV, and the *schedule performance index* (SPI) is the ratio of EV and AC. The performance of your project against schedule can be determined by EVM this way, but **plan variance analysis** is generally a more accurate indicator of schedule performance, and it is easier to evaluate.

The *value* of EVM is debated extensively. It can represent quite a bit of overhead, and for some projects, tracking the data may seem like overkill. On the other hand, EVM accurately predicts project budget overrun as early as 15 percent of the way through a problem project. The project in the figure is about half completed, and it is significantly over budget and somewhat behind schedule.

25 Global Teams – Crosscultural Communication

WHAT: Communicating effectively with distant team members.

WHEN: Throughout a project.

RESULTS: Project communication for international teams that supports project progress.

Effects of Distance and Language

Different primary languages for global team members may make project communication very difficult. Even when team members share proficiency with a written language, spoken communications can cause misunderstandings and lead to problems. Even sharing a language may not be enough; English in different parts of the world uses the same words to describe different things. Project **communication planning** requires minimizing of jargon, acronyms, and idioms, and demands unambiguous content in project documents.

National and regional culture affects communication, but these are not the only forms of culture that can pose challenges. *Company culture* and differences between job functions also matter. How people ask for things, come to agreement, and interact can vary a great deal on any team.

The key to leading projects of all types is communication, and the project leader must ensure *appropriate translations,* so when you are not able to personally provide clear information to the project team and stakeholders, you need to use professional translators. Effective language translation requires both time and money, so consider it in **schedule development,** and include funding for it in your **cost budgeting.** The quality of translation matters, so work to ensure that the translators are competent with both the languages needed and the technology you are working with.

Communication Styles

Global teams also differ in *communication preferences*. While some team members may be more social and talkative, other team members will be more terse and business oriented. Choose **leadership** and communication styles that will work.

Use effective methods of inquiry; *avoid "yes/no" questions* with team members who might respond "yes" to be polite.

Whenever you are asking questions *in writing,* carefully reread them. Even innocently written questions may seem insulting or rude to the people receiving them.

There are no fixed rules on communication styles; the best way to proceed is to establish good **teamwork** and *one-on-one rapport* with distant team members and conduct a face-to-face project **start-up workshop.** That way, minor issues will remain minor and will not escalate into significant problems.

Communication Methods

Communication in global teams is both *formal and informal.* If formal communication (**performance reporting,** documents, scheduled **meetings, presentations,** and **project reviews**) is ineffective, people will have too little information and project performance will suffer. If **communicating informally** (conversations, e-mails, social interactions, and memos) is inadequate, problems will surface too late, when they are difficult to solve. Preferences differ, so balance project communications to support the project and provide communication that serves everyone's needs.

There are *many techniques* for **information distribution,** but on global teams most communication is in the form of either "same time, different place" or "different time, any place." Neither is as effective as in-person communication, but if you conscientiously use all the methods available that are suitable for the team, you can be successful. Avoid using only one or two methods.

Because verbal communication is so difficult on global projects, after teleconferences, meetings, and conversations, always *follow up in writing.*

26 Global Teams – Crosscultural Work Styles

WHAT: Working effectively with team members from other cultures.

WHEN: Throughout a project.

RESULTS: Project performance that meets expectations in all locations where work is done.

Why Global Projects?

Work in modern companies is worldwide. Projects are global for a variety of *reasons*, including:

➤ Products and services are used in many countries.

➤ Companies have employees all over the world.

➤ Global staffing can lower project expenses.

➤ Projects may need skills or knowledge available in different locations.

➤ Alliances and partnerships exist across international boundaries.

➤ New international markets are being opened.

There are many potential *benefits* of global teams:

➤ Access to skills not otherwise available

➤ 24-hour coverage using only people who work a normal shift

➤ Lower project cost

➤ Knowledge of users in many localities

There are also *challenges:*

➤ **Global team communication** is hard, involves multiple languages, and can be expensive.

➤ Time differences are inconvenient.

➤ Work styles and cultural variations can lead to difficulties and misunderstandings.

➤ Confusion and conflict may be frequent.

➤ Effort for global teams is nearly always higher, compared to a co-located team with similar capabilities.

➤ When global teams do get together, it is time consuming and expensive.

The *results* of global projects can be excellent or a disaster (few global projects are "average"), depending on whether the benefits or the challenges dominate. Success requires project **leadership** that minimizes the challenges.

Managing Challenges

Confirm *continuing strong sponsorship.* Lacking adequate **sponsorship of projects,** a global team is almost certain to fail.

On global teams, the *work styles* of team members from different cultures can vary a great deal. Some people are team-oriented and accustomed to working within a defined, structured hierarchy. Other people may be independent and more comfortable working independently in an environment where everyone has equal authority. Strive for a project **scope definition** that decomposes project work in ways that minimize the need for people with different working styles to interact closely. In **project plan development,** structure the work consistently with project staff preferences.

Culture also affects how *time and deadlines* are perceived. Some people are scrupulous about making and meeting time commitments, while others have a less precise approach to deadlines. Even the way that people discuss time varies a great deal, making **status collection** on global teams difficult. Make time commitments as explicit as possible, and minimize dependence for key milestones on team members who have a history of timing problems.

Work to achieve a *consistent view* of the **project vision** and its expected results, and use this to bridge any differences and bring the team together. A common goal that is understood and meaningful to everyone is essential to a smoothly working global team.

Increase **motivation** and buy-in to the project by obtaining *documented commitment* when **delegating responsibility.** Ensure that all managers involved also support and understand the commitments.

Project plan execution also requires *extra attention* on global projects. To be effective, you may need to build **influence without authority.** Inquiries may need to be sent several times, and you generally will send out more information than you get back. Effective project leaders tend to lose some sleep; working with distant team members is most successful when you contact them while they are awake and in the office.

27 Influence Without Authority

WHAT: Gaining commitments from project contributors from other organizations.

WHEN: Project planning, execution, and control.

RESULTS: Cooperative relationships within diverse teams and reliable project commitments.

Prepare

On modern projects, there are many reasons why project leaders may have no direct authority over team members. **Matrix teams,** with contributors who report to other managers, and geographically distributed project teams are prime examples. Projects that depend on staff and consultants external to the project as a result of **procurement planning** may also face control challenges. While cross-organizational teams may have many potential benefits, ultimate project success depends upon your effort and **leadership** to *establish influence,* build **teamwork,** and obtain credible commitments.

One source of influence is **sponsorship** from upper managers or from powerful, respected individuals. Work to *build high-level support* for the project from key decision makers and stakeholders who will back up requests, escalate issue resolution, and assist you in gaining and holding the attention of project contributors. Work with them to establish a **project vision** that they will promote, and align your **project objective** with their goals.

As you assemble the *core project team* and complete your **staff acquisition,** seek team members who are likely to get excited by the project and to be compatible with the rest of the team. Investigate the backgrounds and organizations of potential team members, and discover what they, and their managers, care about.

Plan the **project infrastructure** to best support a diverse team. If the project team is *not co-located,* get committed funding for periodic travel to bring team members face to face. Fully employ **virtual team technical tools** in your **communication planning.** Cultural differences are often both the greatest asset and the biggest challenge for cross-organizational teams. Set up the project to maximize the benefits of diversity, and pay close attention to **global team communication** requirements.

Establish Relationships

Schedule and hold a project **start-up workshop,** so you can get to know your team members better. *Discover the individual preferences* of everyone on the project team. Ask people about recent accomplishments that they are proud of, and probe for their individual goals and aspirations for the project. By discovering what they care about, you can structure project responsibilities to take advantage of their innate **motivation.**

As the planning for the project proceeds, align ownership of work from **activity definition** with individual preferences. When **delegating responsibility,** use the *principle of reciprocity.* In return for a commitment to the project, offer something meaningful in exchange. Assess what you and the project have to offer, and use these currencies to gain reliable agreements to deliver what the project requires. As a project leader, you have more to offer than you may suspect. Currencies for exchange may be:

➤ *Work-related* (significant accomplishment, new skills, working with leading edge technology, access to private information)

➤ *Inspirational* (compelling vision, contribution to an important result)

➤ *Compensating* (**rewards and recognition,** publicity, visibility to management)

➤ *Collaborative* (acceptance, friendship, support)

➤ *Personal* (work preferences, ownership, pride and self-esteem)

Clearly *document all commitments* with team members, and verify each agreement with the team member's direct manager.

Maintain Relationships

Deliver on your promises. Uphold your end of each agreement you have made. Protect your reputation for doing what you said that you would do, fully and on time.

Frequent, effective *communication* is essential to sustaining relationships. Throughout **project plan execution,** tailor formal communications to meet the needs of the team members, and solidify team trust through **communicating informally** with everyone frequently. Meet face-to-face with team members as often as practical. Stay in close contact with team members who belong to external organizations, going beyond the requirements of **contract administration.**

Identify problems before they become project threatening. Be disciplined in **status collection** and use **variance analysis** to detect slipping commitments, so you can quickly recover through **performance problem resolution.** Confront team discord promptly and restore cooperation through **conflict resolution.**

Recognize contributions of team members throughout the project. Thank people individually following completion of project work, and acknowledge communications and status reports. Highlight significant accomplishments, naming names, in **performance reporting** and in project **presentations.**

At least every six months, *assemble the team in person* to reinforce project goals, reacquaint the people, and do a **project review.** Validate all existing and new commitments, and schedule some time for a non-project team-building event to have some fun and celebrate project results so far.

28 **Information Distribution** (PMBOK® 10.2)

WHAT: Providing timely status information to the project team, stake-holders, managers, and others.

WHEN: Throughout a project.

RESULTS: Periodic, accurate reports and presentations, and a thorough, accessible archive for project data.

Routine Project Team Communications

Determine how information will flow within the project, based on the needs, locations of team members, and timing. Do communications planning and select *methods* appropriate for various situations, such as:

	Same place	Different place
Same time	➤ Conversations ➤ Meetings ➤ Networking ➤ Team-building activities ➤ Celebrations	➤ Teleconferences ➤ Videoconferences ➤ Web-based meetings ➤ Telephone calls
Different Time	➤ Reports ➤ Newsletters ➤ Videotapes ➤ Audiotapes ➤ Yellow sticky notes ➤ Memos	➤ Voicemail ➤ email ➤ FAX ➤ Web sites ➤ Network-based tools ➤ Interoffice mail ➤ Other mail

Use all the communication means you have available, and provide informa-tion to team members using the methods they find easiest to use. Team mem-bers will need access to detailed information, so ensure that diagrams, tables, planning documents, and other formatted information can be easily and accurately read, and all communication systems are *compatible.*

Use *standard formats* for routine communications throughout the project to make finding information easier for the recipients. Minimize the use of acronyms, technical jargon, idioms, and other potentially *unfamiliar lan-guage* that may be confusing to some of the project team members. If you must include potentially difficult terminology, define it when you first use it in each document.

Management and Summary Information

When providing high-level project information to project sponsors, managers, and other stakeholders, analyze the information before sending it. Begin with a short *summary* describing the main points you need to communicate. To clarify complicated or technical information, develop graphs, diagrams, and carefully written descriptions to make the information as clear as possible for the people who are not deeply involved with the project. Be careful to exclude unnecessary detail in high-level communications and **presentations.**

Project Management Information System (PMIS)

Decide where and how to *archive project information.* Determine where it will be stored, and for how long. If there are security issues, identify the people who must be able to read and update the archives, and implement systems to ensure that those who should not have access are excluded. Provide for storage of the **project charter,** all project definition reports, project planning documents, and reports and logs that are generated during project execution. If the documents are not stored on-line, develop a system for sending copies to all locations where the project team will access the data, and work to keep all locations synchronized with current versions of each project document.

29 **Integrated Change Control** (PMBOK® 4.3)

WHAT: Managing changes for all project aspects.

WHEN: Project execution and control.

RESULTS: Coherent management of changes, and minimization of unintended change consequences.

Identify Potential Project Changes

Once the **project baseline setting** has been validated, use a set of processes to manage integrated change control for the project. With the plan set and scope frozen, your *documented processes* for dealing with change are essential for project stability and ultimate success. Even for small projects, written processes will enhance your chances of success.

Potential project changes originate from many sources:

➤ *Internal* (**plan variance analysis, performance reporting, project reviews, risk identification,** team-generated ideas, opportunities, loss of staff)

➤ *External* (change requests, regulatory changes, modified standards, **market research,** new technology, meddling sponsors, natural disasters)

For all project changes, the main principle is to *resist all changes* until you can determine that the change represents a net positive business value—that the benefits expected of the change significantly exceed the consequences.

An overall project change process closely resembles the *"Plan-Do-Check-Act"* cycle of quality management. Validate all changes made, and adjust as necessary.

Document and Analyze Changes

Regardless of the source, provide *written documentation* for each proposed change (at a minimum as part of your routine **information distribution**). Scope changes generally employ specialized forms and entail detailed processes for documenting, logging, and tracking submitted changes.

Integrated change control includes many different types of change. *Analyze each proposed change,* using the appropriate process for its type:

Types of Change	Principal Control Processes
Scope	Scope change control, Quality control
Schedule	Schedule control
Cost	Cost control
Procurement	Contract administration
Risk	Risk response planning, Risk monitoring and control
Staffing	Organizational planning
Process	Process improvement, Organizational change
Overall	Project review
Catastrophic	Problem escalation, Canceling projects

Determine the *consequences* for every potential project change in specific terms, such as: cost, timing, effort, reduced deliverable value, staff morale and **motivation,** customer confidence, or other relevant factors. Also consider risks and possible unintended consequences of the change. Change analysis requires the techniques of **project plan development,** especially for major changes.

Estimate the worth of the *expected benefits* of the change (the value of problems solved, shortening of the schedule, improvements to deliverables, higher efficiency, or whatever the primary intention of the change happens to be). Be skeptical of optimistic value assessments for proposed discretionary changes.

Decide and Communicate

Use a systematic process for **decision making,** and make a prompt *business decision* for each change. For each potential change, there are four alternatives: approval, approval with modification, deferral, and rejection. For changes that are mandatory (satisfying legal requirements, solving project-threatening problems, responding to significant external factors), the decision is usually easy: accept the change or cancel the project. For discretionary changes, a default decision of "reject," or at least "defer," is safest, but the net value of some changes may seem so significant that it will make sense to accept them. When this is the case, verify precisely what is necessary and strip out anything superfluous before approving any change.

Before final acceptance of any change that impacts the **project objective, negotiate project changes** and revalidate the project baseline. *Update any project documents* that are affected by accepted changes.

Document every change decision, supported by analysis, and *communicate the results* to team members, appropriate stakeholders, and the originators. Log all change decisions, and store the data in your project information archive, for use in **project reviews** and analysis of **lessons learned.**

Implement all approved changes promptly, and monitor for expected results and any unintended consequences.

30 Leadership

WHAT: Inspiring others toward a shared objective.

WHEN: Throughout a project.

RESULTS: Improved team motivation and enthusiasm, and higher likelihood of project success.

Foundation

Project success depends on effective leadership. Whether you are a program manager with hundreds of people reporting to you, or in charge of a short project staffed by volunteers, or anything in between, you must be a leader. If this is a new role for you, plan for **transitioning to project leadership.** *Identify leadership gaps* and decide what you must do to meet them.

While the role of "manager" can be delegated, you must earn the role of leader from the people you work with. Some of the *critical leadership skills* necessary for this can be developed through practice. Good leaders pay attention, so you must become proficient in active listening. In discussions with others, frequently paraphrase and verify what they have told you, to ensure correct understanding and to let them know you are paying attention. Leaders have credibility, so strive to make your commitments clear and to deliver on what you promise. Effective leaders also display integrity. In your communications, ensure that you consistently say what you mean to say, and that your message is as reliable and factual as you are able to make it.

Lead the Team

Inspire people to get excited about the project. Use techniques for **influence without authority** to identify what matters to your team members. Emphasize aspects of the project that are fun and challenging, and build **motivation** with your enthusiasm and confidence. Projects are complex and difficult. They do not get done because they are easy; they get done because people care.

Understand the values of your team, and work to align your work methods, the **project vision** and **project objective,** and all project communications with these *shared values.* Help people understand why the project is important, through discussions, collaborative planning, and frequent reinforcement of goals and accomplishments.

Develop a *leadership style* that works with your team. Some teams work best under a decisive leader who directs the team autocratically with little input. Other teams prefer **decision making** through unanimous group consensus. Most project teams work best when the style is primarily consensus-oriented, with shifts toward "command and control" as necessary when the team gets stuck or time is critical. In dealing with some team members, it may be necessary to vary your style based on culture, their individual preference, or specific circumstances.

Build *trust and respect* within the team. Develop personal relationships through **coaching and mentoring** with team members, and establish effective **teamwork** among all project contributors. Let people know when you agree with them, and in situations where you may have a difference of opinion, let them know why you disagree in an uncritical, nonthreatening way. Display team loyalty, and initially take the side of your team members in any disputes with others. When you fail to defend the team, your leadership erodes quickly.

Communicate effectively. Keep project documentation up to date and factual. Distribute project reports on schedule. Make time for **informal communication,** and frequently provide acknowledgement and feedback to team members on their work. Encourage each team member to provide you with constructive criticism, and conscientiously decide on any changes you should make to help the project.

Leaders succeed through others. Be generous in giving credit for accomplishments, and *foster a supportive environment* that people will enthusiastically return to for future projects.

Deal with Barriers

Guide **project plan development,** and use realistic information for **project baseline setting.** Resist unnecessary change through scrupulous **scope change control,** and visibly *monitor progress* throughout the project.

Act quickly to *resolve problems* while they are small. In a crisis, you may need to lead as if your authority is greater than your official position. Sometimes leadership requires acting decisively rather than waiting for permission (the "act now, apologize later" strategy). For situations you cannot resolve, do not hesitate to use **problem escalation.**

Be persistent in dealing with project issues. If the first attempt to deal with a problem fails, try again. Successful leaders who embrace difficult assignments often face challenges where multiple failed attempts at solution precede final success. Remember that you can "lose some battles and win the war." Keep your team focused on the overall objectives.

31 **Lessons Learned**

WHAT: Using analysis of current and past projects to improve the processes used for future work.

WHEN: Project execution and closure.

RESULTS: Continued use of good practices and recognition of processes needing attention.

Prepare

Analyzing lessons learned may be done at any time, but it is most commonly performed as part of a **project review** or during **administrative closure** at the conclusion of a project. *Schedule a meeting* for process review soon after a phase of the project completes or the project ends to gather information while it is still fresh in people's memory. Allocate sufficient time for the review. Even shorter projects may generate enough information to justify a half-day retrospective analysis.

Verify that team members and others who should participate will be available, and get their *commitment to attend.* Face-to-face meetings are best, but for **virtual teams,** use the best meeting technology available.

Set a **meeting** *agenda,* including time for:

➤ Positive results: things that went well and practices to repeat

➤ Desirable changes: processes that need improvement or replacement

➤ Prioritization of recommendations

➤ Final thoughts from all contributors

Before meeting, collect accurate, up-to-date *project documents.* For a post-project analysis, ensure that final project reports are available. Also provide access to:

➤ Actual and planned schedule information

➤ Actual and planned resource information

➤ The project **integrated change control** history

➤ Project issues and **problem escalations**

➤ **Project metrics** and **performance reports**

To support analysis of lessons learned, some teams fill out a *survey* in advance, to stimulate thinking about practices to keep or modify and recommendations for change.

Review

Start with a review of the agenda and set the *ground rules* for the meeting. Strive to hear from everyone, roughly equally. Work to identify good practices and opportunities for improvement, not to solve problems on the spot. Keep the focus on project processes—avoid attacking individuals and "blamestorming."

Select a scribe to *capture ideas* generated where all can see them. If the initial scribe was involved in the project, rotate the responsibility for capturing data so everyone can focus on process issues, at least for most of the time.

Probe for *positive aspects* of the project first. Identify specific processes and other project aspects that were successful. Capture what went particularly well on your project; identify new practices that you should repeat or extensions to existing processes that were valuable.

When most of the positives have been listed, shift the focus to *needed changes*. Identify process areas that need improvement and practices that should be simplified or eliminated. If disputes arise, use project documentation and project metrics for **conflict resolution.** Examine issues and problems using **cause-and-effect analysis** to determine root causes, and use **brainstorming** and **process improvement** to generate responses.

During the meeting, *document other issues* or action items that arise that are beyond the meeting scope.

Near the end of the meeting, prioritize the opportunities for improvement using group consensus and *summarize recommendations* for dealing with the most significant ones. If further analysis is necessary, capture action items with owners and due dates.

Close the meeting with reflections on the process. Encourage people to share how they plan to work differently in the future.

Take Action

Document the meeting and list key recommendations and in a clear, short summary followed by the lists of information collected. Distribute the report to the participants and put a copy in the project information archive.

Take action on the *principal recommendations.* Implement any changes where you have the authority, and develop a business case and propose more significant changes to your management. Following every lessons learned analysis, select a project aspect to change that will deal with at least one identified problem.

Monitor changes made, to ensure expected results and no unintended adverse consequences.

32 Market Research

WHAT: Selecting and using techniques for assessing current and future markets for products.

WHEN: Project initiation and planning, with later review as appropriate.

RESULTS: Reliable information for defining project scope and for making sound decisions.

Define the Problem

Market research has many purposes, but the primary use in projects is for **user needs assessment.** Review what you need to learn, and document the *research questions* that you need to answer.

Prior to any new market research, review the *available information.* Check any research done for strategic planning at the organization level. Review internal information such as customer complaints, sales data, and customer requests. Also consider publicly available information from magazines, service bureaus, industry consultants, and the WWW.

Select the Method(s)

For general questions probing for motivations and alternatives, *qualitative techniques* such as **customer interviews,** focus groups, and general surveys are effective.

For testing alternatives, tracking trends, or estimating measurable criteria, *quantitative techniques* are useful; often professional services are employed to design and implement statistically valid models and controlled experiment surveys. You can also use ergonomic testing and prototypes to assess acceptance of new ideas.

Select techniques that will yield the information you require, and develop a plan for the research. Determine who will lead the research effort, and identify the skills and staffing that will be required.

Develop a *proposal* for the research, and obtain approval for the time and funding required. Get agreement on how the results will be used in **decision making.**

Execute Research and Document Results

Execute the research, and interpret the information for use in **scope planning.** File all market research information centrally so other projects can benefit from the information.

Throughout the project, revisit the research as necessary as part of **integrated change control** and for **project reviews.**

33 Matrix Teams (Crossfunctional Teams)

WHAT: Building and maintaining cooperation on project teams where contributors report to different managers.

WHEN: Throughout a project.

RESULTS: Effective teamwork among team members from diverse organizations.

Why Matrix Teams?

Most organizations are organized functionally, and managers are responsible for workers with similar job descriptions—marketing managers manage the marketing staff, and research and development managers are in charge of engineers. In these companies, *complex projects* rely on teams drawn from several functions.

Members of matrix project teams (also called crossfunctional or multidisciplinary teams) have *more than one manager*—their functional manager, plus the person responsible for leading the project. When the project manager has greater authority, the matrix is called strong; when functional managers have more power (the more typical case), it is a weak matrix.

Weak-matrix project teams generally have greater job security and ongoing programs for **team development,** but their commitment to the project and **motivation** may be low. Matrix team projects are often staffed by a group of strangers, so *project leaders* must make the effort to establish **influence without authority** to be successful.

Building an Effective Matrix Team

Techniques for building and maintaining **teamwork** are necessary for matrix teams, but they are not sufficient. Pay *extra attention* to:

➤ Strong project **sponsorship:** intervention by the sponsor may be necessary for **problem escalation** and **conflict resolution.**

➤ Explicit, formal commitments for time and effort from each team member's functional manager

➤ Clearly **delegating responsibility** and defining individual roles, showing precisely why each team member must be on the project

➤ A crossfunctional, thorough process for **project plan development**

➤ A communal space (an actual "war room" or a virtual website location)

Relationships on all project teams are important, but they are more difficult to establish and more quickly destroyed on matrix teams. Identify and take advantage of everything that people on the team do have in common. Start with the **project objective.** Identify the reasons that a successful project is important to each team member, and use it as a foundation for bringing the team together. The most effective way to build a common project vision and trust within the team is to hold a project **start-up workshop.**

High-performing matrix teams also identify and build on *shared personal backgrounds,* such as interests, hobbies, and experiences. Find and build on any past working relationships, especially previous work on successful projects. Personal relationships with mutually respected colleagues may also provide connections.

Doing things together also increases team cohesion. Small group project tasks and non-project team building activities (such as sharing a meal, or events chosen by the team) also contribute to trust.

Create a team identity by *naming the team.* Help people to focus more on the project overall and less on their individual concerns.

Maintaining an Effective Matrix Team

Keeping a diverse team together and motivated depends on intense *loyalty.* Natural loyalties are functional; counterbalance this through unflagging support of team members. Manage **conflict resolution** within the team whenever possible, and deal with **performance problem resolution** one-on-one, resorting to escalation to the individual's manager only as a last resort. While it is difficult, remaining loyal to the team can ensure project success.

Frequent, *effective communication* within the team is also essential. **Communicating informally** is especially important in keeping a crossfunctional team motivated. **Communications planning** for crossfunctional and **global teams** also requires ongoing vigilance in minimizing jargon, confusing technical language, and other sources of potential confusion.

Frequent *personal thanks* to team members for contributions, as well as to their managers, also builds connection to the project. Use available programs for formal **rewards and recognition** to maintain team motivation.

On longer projects, find justification to *bring the team together,* face-to-face, such as **project reviews. Virtual team** members who have little or no personal contact will gradually come to mistrust each other, creating project problems.

34 **Meeting Preparation**

WHAT: A structured process for planning effective meetings.

WHEN: Throughout a project.

RESULTS: Willing attendance at meetings that have business value.

Objective

Effective meetings require preparation. Begin by defining the *meeting objective*. Meetings are costly, so the outcome of any meeting must be valuable enough to justify it.

Based on the meeting objective, determine:

➤ The agenda and topics required

➤ Participants needed and their roles

➤ Meeting logistics

Agenda

Create a draft *agenda* by listing the topics that support the objective. Allow time for starting the meeting, and for reviewing, if necessary, any open issues from previous meetings. Sequence the meeting topics, scheduling the highest priority items first. Allow time at the end to close the meeting. For each *topic*, define the issue, the outcome you expect, the process, and any special roles for participants. On the agenda, list the meeting day, date, starting and ending times, and location.

Whenever possible, send the agenda out before the meeting and ask what the attendees would like to accomplish in the meeting. If the meeting requires advance preparation, discuss the requirements with the participants involved, obtain their commitment, and provide adequate preparation time.

Participants

Meeting *participants* include people who are critical to decisions and recommendations that must be made, people who will be affected by the outcomes of the meeting, and people with knowledge and expertise in the topics that will be discussed. Effective meetings depend on diversity, so involve all necessary people.

Several *roles* are essential for effective meetings, and these are best established before the meeting. Leading an effective meeting requires two roles: facilitation, focused on the meeting processes, and managing, focused on the meeting content. Although one person can fill these two roles, it is generally much more effective to assign these to different people. This is particularly true of large, formal meetings, where the facilitator can keep things on track and serve as a "traffic director" without getting distracted by agenda details. Effective meetings also require a recorder (or scribe) who captures what happens in the meeting.

Logistics

Preparation for effective meetings also includes planning the *logistics*. Ensure that the room is reserved. Verify that the room is large enough and properly equipped. Set up the room in advance, rearranging it if necessary. Plan to bring pens, paper, tape, and any other supplies you may need. Arrange for refreshments if appropriate.

Before the meeting begins, *arrange the room* so that all participants can see the faces of others, as well as any screens or other presentation aids to be used.

If remote participants will be included, arrange for any equipment necessary for **virtual team** telecommunication.

35 Meeting Execution

WHAT: Facilitating efficient meetings and following up afterward.

WHEN: Throughout a project.

RESULTS: Accomplishment of stated meeting objectives and good use of participant's time.

Start the Meeting

First and foremost: *Begin on time.* Waiting for late participants rewards inappropriate behavior and leads to progressively later and later starts.

For small meetings where people do not know each other, begin with *introductions.* For larger meetings, when introductions may not be practical, begin with an interactive "ice breaker" activity.

Start the meeting with a review of the *meeting objectives* and the *agenda* from your **meeting preparation.** Make any necessary adjustments and post the agenda where it is visible. Resolve any details remaining from meeting preparation.

Get agreement on how to run the meeting. If you lack a list of standard *ground rules,* spend a few minutes and develop them. Typical meeting ground rules include:

➤ Attack issues, not people.

➤ Only one person speaks at a time.

➤ No audible pagers, cell phones, or other noise-making hardware are allowed in the meeting room.

➤ Participants take part in discussions by signaling the facilitator, and are recognized in turn.

➤ Everyone has the right to finish speaking.

➤ Everyone has the obligation to be concise.

➤ Written records of the meeting must convey the words of the speakers.

➤ Facilitating and recording roles are rotated periodically.

➤ All participants are responsible for the success of the meeting.

It is never sufficient just to state and post meeting ground rules. The meeting facilitator must also actively enforce them throughout the meeting.

Run the Meeting

Manage time using the agenda to track progress through the meeting. If a topic on the agenda requires more time than planned, bring it to a close and schedule follow-up in a later meeting, or get agreement to revise the agenda. Extend a meeting only as a last resort, and only if the topic is urgent.

Focus on only *one issue at a time.* Whenever a relevant new issue arises, don't ignore it, but don't allow the meeting to get distracted from the current topic. Always record each new issue on a posted "parking lot" or "bucket list" in the meeting room. Avoid disrupting the planned agenda to deal with side issues unless they are truly urgent, but ensure that all topics are dealt with later in the meeting.

Record what occurs throughout the meeting. For each section of the agenda, have a recorder (or "scribe") keep track of what is discussed. If one recorder cannot keep up, have more than one person capture information. Keeping the information legible and accurate aids understanding and allows even latecomers to participate without disrupting the meeting. Discourage paraphrasing that alters a speaker's meaning, and correct the notes whenever any speaker objects to the wording. Throughout the meeting, record decisions, recommendations, and conclusions. Also, record anything that requires further work on a list of "action items." For each action item, clearly define the deliverable(s), assign an owner, and set a target completion date.

Use **conflict management** to deal with problems that may arise during the meeting. Some conflict diminishes if you *enforce the ground rules.* When people interrupt, criticize, or otherwise fail to observe posted rules, deal with this immediately. If your meeting lacks a stated rule for problem behavior, consider taking a moment to add a rule to deal with it. Proactively *confront counterproductive behavior* in meetings. When you fail to deal promptly with inappropriate behavior, it will continue and may escalate.

For longer meetings, schedule frequent *breaks* to keep people engaged. Before each break, announce when the meeting will resume and ask for agreement to return. Always restart the meeting punctually. For meetings longer than an hour, structure the agenda so that the interactions and activities have *variety.* Doing the same thing for too long, especially sitting and listening, is boring and results in ineffective meetings.

Close the Meeting

At the end of the meeting, *deal with the action items,* ensuring that each one is described unambiguously and has an assigned owner and a target for completion. If there are topics that were deferred to the "parking lot" or "bucket" list," decide how you are going to deal with them. If there will be a subsequent meeting with the same group, confirm the date, time, and place, and note any topics that will be on that meeting's agenda. Take time to review what has been accomplished, using the recorder's notes, and end each meeting positively.

It is also good practice to *evaluate* meetings. If you failed to reach any of the intended outcomes of the meeting, briefly discuss why not and what to do about it. Request specific suggestions to improve future meetings, and collect comments on anything in the meeting that went particularly well so you can repeat those things in the future. If necessary, adjust your meeting ground rules.

End the meeting on time or early. Chronically ending meetings late erodes motivation, discourages future attendance, and uses time that should be spent doing other work. Before you leave the room, take a few moments to ensure that it is in good order. Remove used flip charts, erase the boards, dispose of any trash, and restore the seating if you rearranged it.

Follow Up

Based on the notes recorded during the meeting, prepare and distribute a meeting *summary* to the people who attended and others who need to know what happened. Contact any group members who were unable to attend the meeting, especially if they are responsible for any action items.

After the meeting, track the *action items* and follow up on any other business left unresolved, including any items on the "parking lot" list. If there will be a subsequent meeting, begin to prepare for it.

36 **Motivation**

WHAT: Enhancing project team performance.

WHEN: Throughout a project.

RESULTS: Enthusiastic project contributors and successful projects.

Basis

Part of effective project leadership is setting individual goals that people care about. Discover what people want to do and align with their wishes as much as possible when **delegating responsibility.** *Assign ownership* of the work in the project **activity definition** to team members who express interest in it and are good at doing it. Document an owner, by name, for each piece of project work. Involve the owners in analysis, **cost estimation,** and **activity duration estimation** for the tasks to reinforce their ownership and secure their buy-in.

People will be more motivated to deliver on commitments when they receive something in exchange that they desire, so use the *principle of reciprocity* to increase your **influence without authority.**

Measurement drives behavior, so establish and use **project diagnostic metrics** to support the project performance you seek. Motivating measurements are objective, nonthreatening, and used for process improvement, not for punishment.

Build **teamwork** so that people care more about each other and work effectively together to achieve project objectives. *Identify roles* for individuals that draw on their strengths and make them crucial to the project's smooth operation. Understand individual values and establish team values that are compatible.

Establish a *productive environment.* Review the project plan for inefficiency and find opportunities for **process improvement.** Replace or upgrade older equipment, and investigate and deploy more effective methods for communication.

Create an environment of *respect and fairness.* Praise people publicly, but discourage criticism, finding fault, or other negative behavior in front of others. Practice collaborative **decision making,** and encourage participation in **project plan development** and other work. Keep project communications open, bidirectional, and truthful, providing people with the information needed to maintain project progress.

Make the overall project matter. Create a **project vision** that is compelling and that the team vigorously supports. Work together as a team to set high standards for achievement, quality, and excellence that everyone will strive for.

Rewards

Discuss potential **rewards and recognition** for individual and team performance. Tailor rewards and recognition in response to *team preferences*. Use a mix of public and private, tangible and intangible types of positive feedback in response to good performance. Never underestimate the power of intermittent reinforcement.

Frequently identify personal and group accomplishments and *thank people* for them individually. Give credit for significant accomplishments in project **performance reporting,** and when it is culturally appropriate, recognize people for their work publicly in organizational meetings.

Celebrate success. Take time after **project reviews** or at significant project milestones to get the team together and congratulate each other.

In some situations, *monetary rewards* can be motivating. Use them infrequently, to prevent them from becoming expected, and privately, so that they are not demotivating to contributors who do not receive them.

Minimize Demotivating Factors

Promptly deal with *team problems.* Work to detect and deal with missed individual commitments quickly through **performance problem resolution.** When there are disagreements, work within the team to restore cooperation with collaborative **conflict resolution.** For situations beyond your control, promptly use **problem escalation** to request help.

Work to *minimize unnecessary changes* through disciplined **scope change control.** When changes prove necessary, plan your response with the people on the team and work to minimize the disruption.

Identify and *remove valueless project overhead.* Cancel unneeded **meetings** and shorten meetings that are too long. Stop preparing reports that no one reads, and remove activities from the project that are not necessary. Locate and eliminate any other needless work.

37 **Multiple Dependent Projects**

WHAT: Planning projects responsible for independently developed components that are part of a large, complex system.

WHEN: Project planning, execution, and control.

RESULTS: Proactive identification and resolution of project interdependencies and successful complex programs.

Define and Decompose the Program

Program management, responsibility for very large, complex projects begins with overall **scope definition.** As with any project, the goals must align with business strategies and be based on requirements determined through **user needs assessment.** The success of large programs depends on very strong **sponsorship** to get the significant undertaking underway, to deal promptly with complex decisions, and to resolve internal conflicts.

Project management principles alone are not sufficient when work becomes too large and complex, so programs are first logically broken into smaller pieces. The program planning process begins with analysis of overall scope using the principles of **scope definition.** Where scope definition results in a work breakdown structure (WBS) for a project, *program decomposition* results in a number of independent but interrelated projects. Very large programs decompose into a hierarchy of projects, with levels similar to a WBS. The methods used for program decomposition vary with program types, but they include: software architecting, systems analysis, concurrent engineering, and simultaneous development.

Identify the *program staff.* Delegate responsibility for the program as a whole to a program manager. Select owners to lead each of the identified projects of the program, as well as leaders for any intermediate levels in the program hierarchy. Additional program staff, reporting directly to the program manager, may be required for program-level planning, tracking, managing escalations, and reporting. Ensure that the entire program staff is capable of managing their part of a program of this size. Seek staff with skills in high-end **software tools for project management,** facility with complex **communication planning** and management, facility exerting **influence without authority,** and a tolerance for ambiguity.

Get the program off to a *fast start* by conducting one or more program **start-up workshops.** Introduce the overall program objectives and clearly define contributions to the overall goals and the role to be played by each project team.

Plan the Component Projects

The next step in the planning process is **project plan development** for all of the lowest-level projects in the program hierarchy. With awareness of the program objectives and constraints, each project team builds a thorough *bottom-up project plan.*

Because the projects are all interrelated, many of the dependencies for **activity sequencing** will link to other projects. For each project, identify all *required inputs* coming from outside the project that could slow down or stop it.

Document all your *external input dependencies* as program interfaces. You are the consumer who needs the input, so begin a dialog with the leader of the project that you expect will produce it.

Work to *resolve the interface* by requesting commitment from the leader of the producing project.   Focus interface discussions on completion criteria, and obtain an output description for your required input consistent with your requirements. Treat interface agreements as formal contracts. For each of your interfaces, document an agreement between a producer and at least one consumer, including deliverable descriptions and early schedule dates from each project's **schedule development** work.

The program manager or staff will be responsible for *interface management:* coordinating the discussions, escalating and resolving disagreements, locating outputs to match up with unresolved inputs, and formally documenting all program interfaces.

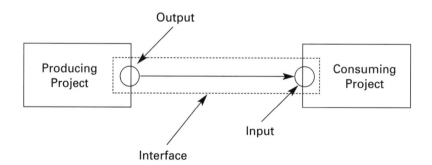

Integrate Plans

If the number of interfaces seems *very high,* it is probably prudent to revisit the initial program decomposition to look for a program structure that has greater project independence. Managing too many interfaces is risky and requires excessive effort.

Create a *program timeline* using data from the interface agreements to show the project connections. Show summary activities for project work (with no detail), and identify dependencies wherever inputs and outputs link the work of two or more projects. Uncover any interruptions or gaps in any of the project schedules.

An initial program schedule rarely meets program timing objectives, and it may also reveal resource overcommitments, budget overruns, and other problems. The program staff and project leaders must work together to develop *alternative project-level plans* using **constraint management and plan optimization** techniques to resolve the program issues. More than one incremental pass may be necessary, especially when working with a hierarchy of projects, adjusting both project timing and **resource planning.** Some problems may require modification of overall program objectives.

Once the overall plans are acceptable to the program sponsor and stakeholders, *document the program baseline* plan.

Track and Manage the Program

Manage project plan execution only for the lowest-level projects in the program. At the program level, *track the interfaces,* variances affecting several projects, and **problem escalations** from the individual projects.

Periodically conduct program and **project reviews** to *revalidate plans* and interface management, especially for lengthy programs.

38 Multiple Independent Projects

WHAT: Managing unrelated projects that depend on shared resources.

WHEN: Project planning.

RESULTS: Predictable execution of all projects and resource planning data supporting organizational decisions.

Plan Each Project

Taking on *too many projects* is a common problem. Good project ideas often exceed the number of projects that can be staffed, and working on all of them is a formula for chaos, low morale, poor **teamwork,** and low **motivation.** Successfully bringing projects to closure requires disciplined attention to detail and concentration on the most critical few.

Focus on *each project individually.* Set a **project objective** and complete **project plan development** one project at a time. Define **activity duration estimates** and complete **schedule development** using consistent units of measure to simplify resource analysis.

Develop resource-loaded schedules for each project based on effort estimates from **cost estimating.** Develop a week-by-week *resource profile,* similar to those used for **resource leveling.** Prepare staffing requirement summaries for each project, both in total and by skill set. Analysis can be automated using resource histograms from a **software tool for project management** or weekly summaries accumulated using a computer spreadsheet.

Develop a second set of resource profiles identifying all available *committed project resources* (overall and by skill set) for each week using the same process you used for your weekly project effort analyses. Take into account holidays, scheduled time off, and other personal conflicts and commitments.

Prioritize the Set of Projects

Use a systematic **decision-making** process to *rank order* all of the projects, based on factors such as the value of the deliverables, urgency, overall importance, strategic contribution, cost, length, or other considerations. If the initial list of projects is lengthy, rank order them first, before developing plans. Create detailed plans for only the top projects that you believe can be staffed.

List the projects in sequence, from the highest priority to the lowest.

Roll Up Resource Requirements into an Overall Resource Plan

Starting with the highest priority project, assign available staff to project activities and summarize the effort profile in a *master resource plan* using a scheduling tool or a spreadsheet.

Continue allocating staff to lower priority projects in sequence, until you add a project that causes the master resource plan to exceed your available resource profile, either overall or for a specific type of contributor. Complete the process by considering smaller projects with slightly lower priorities (if there are any) that could be staffed using remaining resources. Although it is tempting to book all staff fully, it is prudent to leave some capacity uncommitted (up to 10 percent) as a reserve for managing risk.

Adjust Project Objectives

Set the baselines of the highest priority projects and proceed with **project plan execution.**

Negotiate project changes for the remaining projects, based on your resource analysis. Investigate:

➤ *Accelerating the high-priority listed projects* using any uncommitted resources in the master resource profile.

➤ *Obtaining additional resources* to meet the timing and scope objectives of the next several projects on the list

➤ *Extending the deadlines* for the remaining projects, consistent with freeing up of staff after higher priority work completes

➤ *Reducing the scope* for some of the remaining projects so they can proceed

➤ *Outsourcing some work* to increase available staffing

➤ *Replanning the work* on lower priority projects to reduce resource requirements

➤ *Delaying activities on higher priority projects within schedule float* to increase available resources

➤ *Increasing efficiency* through **process improvement,** training, automation, equipment replacement, software upgrades, or other means

➤ *Scheduling overtime,* but only as a last resort

Monitor Progress and Manage Resources

Document the projects that have committed resources and communicate the status of lower priority projects with insufficient resources. Make resource allocation decisions visible, and ensure that sponsors, stakeholders, and team members accept the scheduling decisions.

Track project work by project, and protect work on the highest priority projects.

Manage changes through **integrated change control,** and ensure that the priorities of scheduled work are kept current.

Update the resource profiles and list of current projects periodically, to reflect staffing changes, new project requests, and completed projects.

39 **Negotiating Contracts**

WHAT: Obtaining a formal agreement in a way that leaves all parties involved better off than they would be without the agreement.

WHEN: Project initiation and planning.

RESULTS: Documentation of unambiguous, explicit commitments and a signed agreement that represents value to all.

Prepare

In the course of **solicitation** and **source selection,** learn what you can of the *other party.* Brainstorm their viewpoints and perspectives. Determine who can make commitments for the other party, and always negotiate directly with these decision makers (or with people who are empowered by them).

Document *negotiation objectives* that are important to you. Identify your most important interests, such as completing the statement of work (SOW), cost, or other priorities. Define the worst negation result (such as the highest price or longest schedule) that you can accept. Use your "Best Alternative to a Negotiated Agreement" (BATNA) to define this limit. Be prepared to walk away from a negotiation that fails to meet your preset limits.

Develop a negotiation *strategy.* Include the objectives, prioritized interests, the predefined limits, and criteria for **decision making.** If you lack negotiation experience, seek help from legal, procurement, human resources, or purchasing specialists. Know your own authority, and stay within your negotiating limits.

Before negotiating, *rehearse* your approach. Have someone else role-play the other party and critique you to improve your negotiation strategy.

Conduct Negotiations

Establish a good *working relationship.* You intend to work with the other party after reaching agreement, so strive to build trust. Seek common ground in areas such as interests, experiences, education, or background.

Establish a negotiation *deadline* consistent with the needs of your project, and stick to it.

Communicate honestly and clearly during negotiations. Use facts, data, and metrics to make your points. Clarify your understanding by frequently asking questions and actively listening to what the other party says. Maintain objectivity in lengthy negotiations by scheduling periodic breaks.

Learn what matters to the other party, and relate your discussions directly to these factors. Conduct *principled negotiations* concentrating on the matters that you and the other party most care about. Avoid taking positions that will lead to deadlock, and probe for underlying interests ("Can you help me understand why that is important to you?") when the other party proposes a one-sided solution. When discussions become emotional, acknowledge the situation and then resume using data, or take a break to allow everyone to cool off.

As the negotiation continues, acknowledge areas of agreement, and focus your discussions on any remaining differences. If the negotiations stall, use **brainstorming** to generate possible *alternatives*. Discuss them with an open mind and work to resolve the most significant issues first. If it becomes obvious that there can be no mutual agreement meeting your criteria, terminate the negotiation.

Reserve final agreement until all the issues are resolved, but *document specifics* of deliverables, completion criteria, costs, timeliness, penalties, and other important criteria as you proceed. For each deliverable, ensure that specifications, ownership, and timing are very clear. Discuss all acceptance and testing criteria, and establish procedures for **scope change control.** Negotiate terms that support your project; align any payments with achievement of specific results.

Close Negotiations

Once you reach an acceptable *final agreement,* document it in writing using plain language. Whenever possible, use a standard format or preprinted form to capture the essential points of your agreement.

Acknowledge the accomplishment and express appreciation to the other party.

Finalize and Implement

Complete the agreement by obtaining *authorized signatures* from individuals representing each party. Process necessary paperwork and begin **contract administration.**

40 Negotiating Project Changes

WHAT: Using bottom-up project planning data to gain support for necessary changes in project objectives.

WHEN: Project planning, execution, and control.

RESULTS: Modified expectations for the project that are consistent with a credible plan.

Assemble Your Data

The results of your **project plan development** may fail to support the **project objective,** even after your best efforts at **managing constraints and plan optimization.** When this happens, *assemble factual data* from your bottom-up planning process and prepare to negotiate project changes with your project sponsor. Include:

➤ *A high-level* plan summary with a milestone project schedule

➤ The *work breakdown structure* from **scope definition**

➤ A *Gantt chart* or other schedule showing project timing

➤ *Resource and budget summaries* from **resource planning**

➤ One or more *proposals for alternative projects*

Build a case demonstrating that the *initial project objective is infeasible* using your planning data. Gaining agreement to necessary project changes requires fact-based, principled negotiation. Sponsors have more power and authority than project leaders and may easily dismiss arguments based only on your concerns or opinions. Negotiations lacking plausible data will likely fail.

Practice

Develop your *negotiation objective.* Decide what you wish to accomplish from the negotiation, and document it. If you need more time, or more resources, build a good business case to support your request. If changes to the project deliverable seem necessary, show why, and be able to demonstrate the value of the modified result. Develop project alternatives that provide for mutual gain, such as exploring opportunities that could extend beyond the original project request, or segmenting the project into a sequence of smaller projects that might deliver value earlier. Prepare compelling **presentations** to support your proposals, using unambiguous, nontechnical language.

Before setting up a meeting with your sponsor, *rehearse* what you will say. Ask a team member to pretend to be your sponsor, and go through your case for change. Seek criticism, and use it to improve your negotiation approach.

Negotiate

Schedule a meeting with the project sponsor to discuss the results of your planning, and your alternative plan or plans.

Begin your discussions by showing how the *best planning results* are inadequate for achieving the initial project goals. Use your planning summary, supported by additional detail as necessary.

Present your *best alternative*, along with any other good options you developed. Encourage questions and discussion of alternatives, and support your proposals using historical, documented project data.

Strive for *"win–win" negotiations*, in which both you and your sponsor get a good result. In project negotiations in which only the sponsor "wins," everyone loses. If the objective is impossible, the project team loses because they will be stuck on a doomed project, and sponsors and project stakeholders lose too, because they will not get what they expect.

Use your planning alternatives to guide discussions toward *problem solving* and get everyone involved in seeking better options. Focus negotiations on resolving project issues. Work to shift the project objective in line with a realistic plan.

Close the Negotiation

Request agreement for a project objective that you can execute using a realistic plan. Following agreement, you can use the plan for **project baseline setting.**

If a realistic analysis of your best project plan leads to recognition that the project is a bad idea, *take it no further.* Canceling doomed projects early is better for everyone.

If your presentation fails to convince your sponsor or falls on deaf ears, you might be forced into an *infeasible project*. If so, document the situation for future reference, and then see if you can find a way out of the project.

41 **Organizational Change**

WHAT: Modifying how people do their work.

WHEN: As necessary.

RESULTS: Support for a needed process change, with minimal resistance and prompt adoption.

Document the Need

When **project metrics** reveal an *ineffective process* (as part of **performance reporting, quality control, project reviews,** or **lessons learned**), use **process improvement** techniques to develop a better method and to document a new standard operating procedure.

Unless the new process is completely automated, developing a new process is only part of the job; you must also provide **leadership** to *gain acceptance* for the new way of working and convince people to switch from the old process.

Define Roles

Effecting change in an organization depends on a number of roles:

➤ *Advocates*—Project leaders often advocate project process changes. As an advocate, you recognize a need for change, develop a business case, and use **consensus building for your ideas** to gain sponsorship.

➤ *Sponsors*—Project changes are generally sponsored by managers of project leaders, after advocates show that change is desirable.

➤ *Agents*—Change agents manage the project to develop and introduce the new process.

➤ *Targets*—The individuals who are affected by the change need to be persuaded to modify how they work.

Plan for Change

Develop a plan for implementing the change, including four key elements:

➤ Outline *sponsor* responsibilities, and get commitments for sending memos, leading meetings, and other contributions.

➤ Develop *objective metrics* that define the initial process baseline and can be used to demonstrate the results of the new process.

➤ Describe *success stories* from earlier, similar efforts (such as a pilot) to persuade the people who are the target of the change to cooperate.

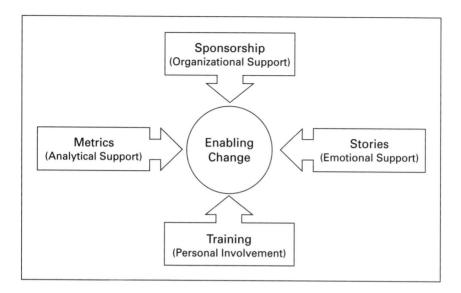

Prepare the target users for the change through *training*, and involve them in planning for the change.

Get funding for the communication, training, and other costs of the transition, and set realistic expectations for the rate of change. Significant changes may take six months or longer to be fully integrated into normal operations.

Implement the Change

Persuade the people affected of the benefits of change. Clearly demonstrate "What's in it for me" from their perspective. Build **motivation** for the change.

Use metrics to measure the initial results of the change. If the **project diagnostic metrics** fall short of expectations, or there are any significant unintended consequences, be prepared to modify the process as necessary to improve it further, or to restore the old process.

Reinforce cooperation and successful change. Develop **rewards and recognition** for target users who embrace change, and develop additional success stories using their experiences to support later phases and to improve change acceptance by people who are lagging behind.

Continue efforts throughout the transition, until process measurements indicate you have achieved your objective. At the conclusion of the change effort, analyze the project **lessons learned** and make recommendations that will *improve future change efforts*.

42 **Organizational Planning** (PMBOK® 9.1)

WHAT: Defining roles, responsibilities, and organizational structures for the project.

WHEN: Project initiation and planning.

RESULTS: A project roster defining expected contributions and reporting relationships, either by name or with a plan for resolving staffing requirements.

Review Staffing Procedures and Standards

For projects that will *need to add staff* through hiring, employee transfer, contracting, or other means, ensure that you understand the processes required and that you have commitment from your project sponsor and others in your organization who must support and approve the process. Locate and use templates, filled-out forms, and other staffing documents to minimize effort and potential problems in moving forward.

Identify the *support people* in your organization (such as legal, procurement, and human resources) who will be involved, and obtain their commitment to assist your project.

Determine Skill and Effort Requirements

Assess the overall project needs for organizational support and communication, technical inputs, stakeholder management, user and customer interaction, and other necessary relationships. Document these *interfaces,* liaisons, and connections and determine how the project staff will manage them.

As part of project **resource planning,** perform **required skills analysis** to determine the skills, knowledge, and experience levels required for necessary project work. Determine the project effort requirements through **cost estimating,** based on the timing and anticipated staffing of the work. Initial staffing is based on "rough order of magnitude" (ROM) analysis and estimating. Document project *staffing needs.*

Develop a Project Roster

Outline the roles and responsibilities required by the project work, and determine the number of project contributors needed for each of the roles. For each identified role for which there is a capable team member already committed to the project, *list the contributor by name* in a project roster or organization chart, along with contact information and other needed data. When project contributors are also committed to other projects or to nonproject work, determine and document the amount of effort available, and include their availability in the overall staffing analysis. Some find it useful to distinguish between "core" project team members, assigned to the project full time throughout the work, and "extended" team members, who are essential but less involved.

For roles that are not filled (or only partially filled), decide how best to *meet the need*—using additional people already in the organization, external staffing, or some other means.

Plan for Staffing

If there are unmet staffing requirements, explicitly plan for **staffing acquisition.** Develop a *staffing plan* to fill team positions using hiring or internal staff. Execute **procurement planning** to fill staffing needs best met with external staff. As part of the planning process, compare the staffing costs with **project objectives** for expense, and prepare to **negotiate project changes** if there are significant differences.

43 Organizing for Project Management

WHAT: Defining and implementing the foundation for effective project management.

WHEN: Prior to the project and project initiation.

RESULTS: An environment for successful projects.

Project Management Support

Maximizing the effectiveness of project management processes requires a combination of organizational will and well-defined, consistent methods. If your environment lacks elements outlined here, look for ways to establish them.

Some attributes of high-performing project management organizations include:

➤ An effective *project manager selection process.* There are few "accidental" project managers in these organizations, because they appoint project leaders based on what they know an individual needs to have for successfully **transitioning to project leadership.**

➤ *Ongoing support and interest by higher-level managers* (but not day-to-day involvement). Strong **sponsorship of projects** is crucial in avoiding the problems of "too many projects," "decision delays," and "resource erosion." Sponsors who initiate projects and then lose interest in them set them up to fail.

➤ Readily available *project management training,* mentoring, and support. Competent project management develops more quickly in these companies.

➤ *Project-oriented recognition programs.* **Rewards and recognition** are structured to encourage **teamwork,** not individual acts of heroism.

Project Management Methods

Well-defined *methods and processes* for project management are also essential. The method that you choose matters less than that you document, adopt, and consistently use a process that supports thorough **project plan development** and competent **project plan execution.**

Project processes are necessary but may not be sufficient. The *other methods,* life cycles, and development techniques used must align and support your project processes. If your latest fad for software application development is based on the concept that thinking and planning represent unnecessary overhead, projects will fail.

Project metrics, stored in an organization-wide *project management information system,* also contribute to project excellence. Better estimating, more thorough **risk identification,** and shared templates of planning information are all valuable intellectual assets.

A final ingredient for maximizing project success is a process to directly *align project objectives and organizational strategies.* Formal coupling of projects to visible, high-level objectives will protect resources, ensure priority, and remove barriers, significantly improving the chances of project success.

44 Performance Problem Resolution

WHAT: Promptly recognizing unmet individual goals and resolving them.

WHEN: Project execution and control.

RESULTS: Consistent delivery on commitments while maintaining motivation and self-esteem.

Identify the Situation and Probable Causes

When project **status collection** or other communication reveals that an individual goal has been missed or is in jeopardy, identify the problem and outline the consequences to the project (in schedule slippage, budget overrun, or other adverse results). Consider possible root causes for the situation, which may include:

➤ **Delegating of responsibility** and ownership is unclear.

➤ The individual lacks knowledge, skill, or aptitude for the work.

➤ The individual has more work to do than can be accomplished.

➤ There are insufficient resources to complete the work.

➤ The work is dependent on an input that is late.

➤ **Information distribution** regarding the work is inadequate.

➤ The individual is from another organization, where the priority of the work and commitment are low.

➤ There are no **rewards or recognition** tied to achieving the goal.

➤ There are no visible **project diagnostic metrics** associated with the activity.

Confront the Problem

Meet, face-to-face if possible, with the individual to discuss the situation. Reconfirm the commitment to the goal, reviewing the expected results, timing, and other specifics. Outline the consequences of missing the commitment, emphasizing the ones that affect the individual personally.

Discuss the *cause of the problem.* Start by allowing the project contributor to describe the reasons in his or her own words. Probe for the root cause, not just a surface rationalization.

Develop *possible solutions,* again beginning with suggestions from the individual. Seek solutions that align with the root cause: **team development** such as training or **coaching and mentoring** for a skill gap, or **problem escalation** to resolve a delayed input or resource shortage. After the team member has had an opportunity to suggest a path forward, offer your own suggestions.

Agree on Next Steps

Select an option that will mitigate or solve the problem, and document it.

Get the individual's agreement and *commitment* to follow through, and express your confidence in his or her ability to deliver. Revise the specifics of any affected goals and update your project plans as necessary.

Implement and Track

Track progress toward recovery of the goals.

Explicitly *recognize improvements* by thanking the individual (and his or her manager, if it is not you) for improved performance.

If problems persist, meet again. If several cycles yield no improvement, consider alternative ways to meet your project's requirements, or, as a last resort, escalate resolution of the situation to your project sponsor or management.

45 **Performance Reporting** (PMBOK® 10.3)

WHAT: Formally documenting project performance against the baseline plan.

WHEN: Project execution and control.

RESULTS: Visible tracking of project results compared with expectations.

Assess Progress

Performance reporting is central to **project plan execution.** It is the final part of the project tracking cycle, following **status collection, plan variance analysis,** and if necessary, actions for project recovery. Before documenting project performance, *verify status* of significant variances in schedule, cost, and other project metrics, and ensure that all project actions are consistent with:

➤ Integrated change control

➤ Scope change control

➤ Cost control

➤ Schedule control

➤ Quality control

➤ Project priorities

Review Performance

Use **project diagnostic metrics** such as **earned value management** to *measure project performance.*

Periodically, such as during **project reviews,** *analyze trends* in project data to identify potential issues, poorly performing processes, and potential project risks.

Report Performance

As defined in **communications planning,** prepare a *written status report.* Reporting is most effective when it is neither too cursory nor too rambling. Both too little and too much information result in confusion and loss of project control. Confine your reporting to factual information and be consistently honest, even regarding bad news.

Adopt a standard reporting format, and always begin with a *short executive summary.* Limit it to about one-half page, and include a list of no more than seven brief descriptions of key project accomplishments, next steps, and issues. Make the summary clear; some of the people who get your report will read no further.

Follow your summary with *additional information,* in order of relative importance. Customize reporting for different audiences by truncating the less essential information rather than by rewriting. A typical project status report may include:

➤ The executive summary of accomplishments, plans, and issues

➤ Status of change requests

➤ A schedule summary, with planned, actual, and expected future dates

➤ A resource summary, with planned, actual, and expected future resource requirements

➤ A detailed project analysis, including an explanation of any variances

➤ Risk reporting, including status of ongoing risk recovery efforts

➤ Additional detail, charts, and other information as needed

Always *proofread your report* for errors, omissions, and unclear language. Correct any problems, and replace technical jargon, acronyms, and idioms with terminology that all the readers will understand.

Send the report to team members, appropriate stakeholders, and others as part of project **information distribution.** Archive all reports for later reference and use them in analyzing **lessons learned.**

46 Plan Variance Analysis

WHAT: Identifying differences between baseline plans and actual performance.

WHEN: Project execution and control.

RESULTS: Prompt recognition of project performance problems and issues.

Verify Status

Plan variance analysis is central to **project plan execution.** It follows **status collection** in the project tracking cycle. Before beginning to analyze variance, *validate* the status information. Check it for completeness, consistency with past data, and credibility compared with other current status and project information.

Determine Variances

Compare the status reported with the **project baseline.** Note all *differences,* both beneficial and adverse. Positive variances may provide options for project acceleration, and even small negative variances deserve your prompt attention while they are still manageable. Determine the overall effect of any changes, issues, problems, and risks to the project schedule and budget.

Schedule variances are generally the most visible. Note all work that is completed either early or late. For continuing activities expected to finish late, forecast the delay. Determine variances for all current activities, not just critical ones.

Assess any *resource variances,* noting differences between resource estimates and actual results. For **earned value management,** determine the baseline for variance analysis each cycle using a consistent method, such as the "50/50" rule (assuming half of the estimated cost at activity start, and the remainder at the end).

Also note any *other variances,* such as performance issues related to project scope.

Analyze Impact

For each variance, determine the *impact* on the project. For positive schedule or budget variances, investigate to see whether estimates for future project work might also be larger than necessary. For negative differences, determine how the project is affected.

For each timing delay, estimate the *schedule impact* (if any) on project milestones and the deadline. Even for non-critical activities, use **cause-and-effect analysis** to determine the root cause of each slip. Similar optimistic estimates may recur later in the project, resulting in delays in finishing other work.

Determine the overall *budget impact* of any resource variances. Unlike schedule variances, all resource variances affect the project; every effort or **cost estimate** that is too low contributes to budget overrun. Even early in the work, an excessive money or resource "burn rate" is a strong predictor of budget problems. It is very difficult to reverse resource overconsumption.

Assess the *overall impact* of other variances from the project baseline plans and objectives. If results of tests, feasibility studies, or other work fall below expectations, determine how they are likely to affect the project. Significant variances may result in:

➤ Scope changes

➤ Schedule slippage

➤ Increased budget or other resource requirements

➤ Impact on other projects

Trend Analysis

Trend analysis is not necessarily part of each tracking cycle, but it is useful to examine the trends in the status data at least during **project reviews.** Use trend analysis to detect budget, schedule, and other problems as *early in the project* as possible. If trend analysis reveals a need for **negotiating project changes,** such as the project end date, the budget, staffing, or project deliverables, deal with this as soon as possible. The earlier you propose needed changes, the more likely you will be to get support and agreement. Waiting too long to confront trends often leads to **canceling projects.**

Document Findings

Probe for the root cause of each significant variance, and document both the *source and impact* of each problem for use in **schedule control, cost control, performance reporting,** and overall project problem resolution.

47 **Presentations**

WHAT: Organizing, summarizing, and formally presenting project status.

WHEN: Project execution and control.

RESULTS: Broad awareness of project progress, accomplishments, issues, and future plans.

Define

Clearly outline the *purpose* of the presentation. State your objective for the **meeting** and the reasons why the presentation is necessary. Some presentation objectives include **project review** summaries, **problem escalation,** phase or stage-gate transitions, and final project reporting.

Determine *who will be attending* the presentation and find out what about your project matters most to them. Identify issues and questions that they are likely to want addressed. Invite them, and confirm their attendance.

Schedule the presentation at a time that is convenient for the attendees. Decide how you will provide information in the presentation: projected slides, prepared posters or charts, handouts, or other media. Reserve a place for the meeting (or for a distributed audience, the network, and telecommunications facilities) and determine that the presentation method chosen is appropriate.

Prepare

Set an *agenda* for the presentation, including introductory material, specific content covering all necessary areas, time for questions and discussion, and a conclusion. Start by telling what you will tell them, tell them, and end by telling them what you told them.

Organize all the project information that you intend to include into a logical sequence. If the information is detailed and complex, analyze it and work to summarize the content using graphs, tables, and simple bulleted lists. Keep lists and presentation slides short—four or five listed points maximum, using large-size lettering. Add interest to presentations using relevant figures, pictures, and some color, but don't overwhelm your message with clip-art. For necessary material that is more complex, prepare a supporting handout, and consider distributing it in advance.

Develop an opening for your presentation that focuses the group's attention. If the group attending is small, use individual introductions or group

brainstorming. For larger groups, "break the ice" using an appropriate humorous story or a thought-provoking question.

Edit your presentation, repairing errors and potentially confusing text. Prepare no more than about one presentation slide for every five minutes, and keep the overall length to a minimum. Leave at least ten minutes of planned time in the presentation for questions and discussion.

If you need any markers, sticky notes, paper, or other *supplies,* get them in advance or ensure that the meeting place is well stocked with what you need.

Rehearse

Practice your presentation in advance for at least one other person. Work on smoothly saying what you need to say to support any visual slides, providing explanations and transitions without reading the text verbatim. If you prepare a script, use it only as guidance. Practice saying your message naturally, the way you normally speak.

Get feedback on your *body language.* Much of your message is conveyed by your speech patterns, gestures, and attitudes. Work on maintaining a positive, friendly demeanor, and keep eye contact with the people attending the presentation. If you plan to demonstrate or use something complicated, practice it until you can do it without having to think about it consciously.

Make adjustments to your presentation based on the feedback you receive.

Deliver

Arrive early, and *begin on time.* As people arrive, greet them and thank them for attending. After you open your presentation with an introductory activity or a story, review your agenda.

Present your content confidently and efficiently, pausing for questions as appropriate. Move around during the presentation and vary your delivery to avoid monotony. Ask questions every few minutes that relate to your presentation to keep people involved. Resist becoming defensive or emotional in reaction to what people say or ask; use humor and factual data to restore order.

Close with a *summary* of what you have said. Capture any open issues or questions that came up, and commit to responding promptly. Thank everyone for attending and end the presentation on time.

48 **Problem Escalation**

WHAT: Delegating responsibility for resolution of decisions, differences, issues, and conflicts upward.

WHEN: Throughout a project.

RESULTS: Timely resolution of situations impeding a project that are beyond the influence of the project team.

Establish the Escalation Process

Develop a process for problem escalation consistent with your organizational policies, expected project requirements, and your **project infrastructure.** Identify when the process is to be used, expectations for timing, and who is responsible for responding to escalation requests. *Document* the process in clear language.

Get explicit *commitment* for the process during **project initiation** from the project sponsor, key stakeholders, and any others who may be involved in escalation responses. Reconfirm commitment to the process periodically during **project reviews.**

Escalate as a Last Resort

Attempt resolution using *other options* first, such as:

➤ Performance problem resolution

➤ Conflict resolution

➤ Influence without authority

➤ Decision-making process

➤ Negotiating project changes

If the problem persists even after your team's best efforts, *document* a summary of the problem. Include the results of all of your attempts to deal with it.

Outline *possible approaches* for solution that might be available to others with more authority, including any that you may not necessarily favor. Quantify the costs and other consequences of these alternatives as thoroughly as you are able. Also quantify any consequences of failing to resolve the problem promptly.

Provide the data to your sponsor or some other appropriate decision maker in your organization. Assign a due date for a response, and get explicit commitment of ownership from the decision maker.

Track the status of the escalation as an action item in your project **performance reporting,** explicitly assigned to the decision maker. Continue tracking until you receive a response. If there is delay, report the status and name names.

Implement the Response

Implement the decision made, managing any major project shifts using **integrated change control.** Do your best to minimize adverse project costs or consequences, and work to repair any bruised relationships.

49 **Process Improvement**

WHAT: Identifying and developing beneficial changes in processes used to do recurring work.

WHEN: Throughout a project.

RESULTS: More effective, efficient work methods.

Plan

Identify a poorly performing process (for example, through **quality control, quality assurance, performance reporting, project reviews,** or **lessons learned**).

List the problems and defects of the process. Discuss the situation within your team and with others affected. *Gain support* for a process change effort through **consensus building for your ideas.**

Assign an owner to manage the improvement project, and plan the project, defining the time, staffing, and other resources necessary for the improvement effort. Set a deadline and quantify the improvement target. Verify management *commitment* to the work required.

Baseline

Describe the *current process* using a system flowchart map or a detailed description of the present standard operating procedure (SOP). List the inputs and outputs for the process and the circumstances that trigger its execution. Use **cause-and-effect analysis** to identify the root causes of problems with the "as-is" process.

Gather data on the current process through interviews, project **status collection,** observations, and trend analysis. Document the *measurement baseline* for the present situation, and validate your quantified performance improvement goals against it.

Develop Changes

Analyze the "as-is" process and develop *options for a new process:*

➤ Inspect the process for work that adds little or no value.

➤ Identify decisions and branches in the process that are unnecessary or too late in the process.

➤ Find opportunities to reduce or eliminate rework.

- Consider automating repetitive process steps.
- Refine inputs or process steps to minimize effort.
- Devise ways to reduce or eliminate process loops.
- Consider methods that increase process flexibility.

List the options you found, and select the most promising alternatives. *Describe the "to-be" process* that incorporates these changes.

Present the new process to your stakeholders and get *approval* to proceed with replacement of the old process. Apply **integrated change control** principles.

Implement

Document a new SOP, using system flowcharting and written descriptions. Create any reference documentation, training, or other supporting materials needed. Develop a clear description of the benefits and objectives for all those affected.

Introduce the new process using good **organizational change** practices, and put the new process into practice.

Measure Results

Measure the results obtained using the new process, and compare them with the original process baseline and your improvement goals. If the goals have been met and there are no significant unintended consequences, close the project.

If your changes *fail to meet* the goals or the new process displays unacceptable consequences, analyze the situation and fix the process using further changes, revert to the old process, or try again with a new process improvement project.

50 **Procurement Planning** (PMBOK® 12.1)

WHAT: Determining whether to outsource project work.

WHEN: Project initiation and planning.

RESULTS: Analysis of costs and benefits, a defined statement of work, and good procurement decisions.

Review Project Information

Inspect the **scope definition** to identify activities in the project *work breakdown structure* that are candidates for outsourcing. Review your **required skills analysis** and **resource planning** information to determine whether there are skill gaps on your team or portions of the project with resource shortfalls.

Before beginning to consider contracting project work out, review the process your organization uses for procurement. Familiarize yourself with all of your available sources of *procurement expertise*. Identify all the individuals who will need to be involved; other resources you will need; and all the forms, approvals, and communication required.

Make versus Buy

Evaluate *issues* related to project activities that may be outsourced:

➤ Will outside work be more expensive than internal?

➤ Does the work involve anything proprietary, confidential, or related to a competitive advantage?

➤ Will it be difficult to define the expected deliverables precisely enough to avoid integration problems?

➤ Does the work required involve one of your core competencies?

➤ Are changes in the specifications unlikely?

➤ Will there be someone on the project team with the time and expertise to manage the solicitation and contracting process, serve as liaison, review outsourced work, and approve payments?

Outline any expected *benefits* of outsourcing:

➤ Access to otherwise unavailable skills and expertise

➤ Faster execution by increasing the amount of work in parallel

➤ Advantages resulting from use of specialized equipment or other capabilities that will not be needed after the project.

Consider the *risks* of outsourcing:

➤ Outsourcing work involving new technology or methods may cause staff **motivation** problems and erodes **team development.**

➤ Delays and problems may be hard to detect in advance.

➤ Staff turnover in contracting organizations may result in delays and excessive "learning curve" overhead.

➤ Communication problems and misunderstandings are more likely.

➤ There are high penalties for imprecise early planning and changing design specifications.

➤ Finding and qualifying vendors may take more time than you have.

➤ Contracting for any required follow-on work may be impossible or expensive.

➤ Selecting the lowest-cost proposal may result in quality problems.

➤ Confidential information may be exposed.

Weigh the issues, benefits, risks, probable costs, and other factors. Determine whether to outsource based on solid *business criteria* and good **decision making.** Avoid contracting out project work based only on the lack of available staff.

Document

For all project activity that you intend to outsource, develop a thorough *statement of work* (SOW), including detailed feature specifications, deliverable performance and acceptance criteria, any other relevant requirements, and the necessary timing. Ensure that the SOW is consistent with your project **scope planning.** Develop a rough estimate of anticipated cost.

Consider contracting options (such as fixed price or time and materials) and describe how you will decide which to recommend. Determine how many proposals you will need to consider. Develop a *procurement management plan*, consistent with your organizational practices. Identify timing and staffing for all necessary work.

Get Approval

Present a summary of your SOW, supporting business data, and your procurement plans to your project sponsor. Be prepared to support the summary with your detailed data. *Obtain approval* to initiate the **solicitation** process and funding commitment for the expected expense.

Initiate contact with contracting, legal, human resources, or other *procurement specialists* who will be needed in the process. Get their commitment to support your procurement efforts.

51 **Project Baseline Setting**

WHAT: Committing to a project plan based on bottom-up project information.

WHEN: Project planning and execution.

RESULTS: A solid basis for project tracking and control, with project expectations, deadlines, and budgets aligned with reality.

Review Plans and Objectives

Setting the project baseline is the *final component* of **project plan development.**

Assemble your project plan components and verify that the planning is thorough, realistic, and capable of delivering the results desired. Inspect your plans for omissions, excessive optimism, and other defects. Compare the total number of effort months required by your project plan with the effort actually used to finish several similar earlier projects successfully. Adjust your estimates and plans if the comparison seems too optimistic. Ensure that **project reviews** are scheduled periodically on long projects.

Identify any issues between your plan and the initial **project objective,** in terms of timing, budget, staffing, or other stated goals. If there are significant differences or project constraints that are not consistent with your plans, work to remedy them through **constraint management and plan optimization.**

If the result of your best bottom-up planning still fails to meet key goals of the project, prepare *several plan variations* that do deliver on the highest **project priorities.**

Prepare

Summarize the data from planning to present to your project sponsor. Include an executive summary of the plan, as well as resource and cost analysis, schedule, risk plans, and other pertinent information. Presentation of great volumes of planning information may be more distracting than helpful, so plan to bring detailed information along mainly for reference.

If you will be **negotiating project changes** before setting a baseline, prepare to *justify necessary modifications* with credible information, and develop two or more proposals outlining realistic projects with solid business cases.

Set up a meeting with your sponsor, requesting sufficient time to discuss the project and gain agreement on your plans. Before the meeting, practice your **presentation** with a team member or two and encourage their criticism. Following the planning process, you are the world authority on your project; rehearse your presentation until you confidently sound like it. Work to improve your presentation, and use your strengths: your project experience, your background and skills, and your enthusiasm for the project.

Set the Baseline

Meet with your sponsor and present your project data.

When it is necessary, *shift project objectives* using fact-based negotiation and **consensus-building for your ideas.** Convince project sponsors and stakeholders to support a project that makes sense and serves everyone's interests.

Following presentation of the project plans, seek agreement on a specific deliverable, a resource commitment, and a deadline, all consistent with a feasible plan. *Validate the plan* and verify that the resulting objective is acceptable both to the project sponsor and to your project team.

Set the baseline plan of record using your project plans.

➤ *Publish the final versions* of the project documents.

➤ *Communicate plans* and arrange for distribution and access by the project team, online if possible.

➤ *Save a baseline schedule* if you are using a **software tool for project management** and begin tracking status in the database.

➤ *Freeze all specifications,* and begin **integrated change control** and **scope change control.**

Manage the Project Baseline

Use the project baseline for **project plan execution.** Structure **status collection** with it, and use it as the foundation for **performance reporting.**

Never change a baseline without using your change control processes, and keep track of any modifications made during the project.

Compare the baseline with actual results during project reviews and for analysis of **lessons learned.**

52 **Project Charter**

WHAT: Developing a high-level project description to launch a project formally.

WHEN: Project initiation and planning.

RESULTS: A reference document used to guide project planning and staffing.

A project charter is a *formatted collection of information* assembled as a part of **project initiation** or soon afterward. Because projects may differ, this documentation may also be known as a:

➤ Project definition document

➤ Project datasheet

➤ Proposal

➤ Reference specification

➤ Statement of work

➤ Plan of record

Whatever the project description documentation is called, the important thing is that it be written down.

Collect Inputs

Review information from the **sponsor of the project,** including the business need, problem statement, or other rationale for the project. Summarize the desired results and goals, constraints and assumptions, and initial project staffing information. Document the business standards and organizational requirements relevant to the project.

Develop the Charter

A project charter begins with the *sponsor.* For charter information provided by the sponsor, review each part and validate your understanding of the information.

Charters vary in specific *content,* but most include:

➤ **Project objective** statement

➤ **Project priorities**

➤ High-level scope statement, describing all expected deliverables

- Description of the expected users or customers
- The business case for the project (benefit or **return on investment analysis**)
- Rough cost estimates
- Target milestones and deadlines
- Project leader and initial staffing information
- Identified dependencies
- Key constraints and assumptions
- Known issues and high-level risks

Document and Distribute

Validate the content of the charter with the project sponsor and stakeholders.

Add the charter to the project information archive, and provide it to the project team and stakeholders *in writing.* Putting the charter on-line is best, but if it is on paper, set up a process for updating and replacing it following any necessary changes.

Use the charter as a basis for **scope planning,** other **project plan development** activities, and **project reviews.**

53 Project Infrastructure

WHAT: Establishing a framework for project planning and control.

WHEN: Project planning, execution, and control.

RESULTS: Documented decisions ensuring comprehensive planning and efficient project execution.

List Key Decisions

Infrastructure planning provides a *foundation* for planning, execution, and control. Documenting infrastructure decisions clarifies how the project will operate. Infrastructure planning varies in length from a few hours to several days of effort, depending on project scale.

Begin infrastructure planning early in a project by reviewing **project initiation** information, the **project objective,** and other available documentation such as the **project charter.** Make infrastructure decisions early; mid-project structural change is difficult.

Create a list of *infrastructure decisions.* Model your list on the sample list that follows, or one from an earlier project, or a suitable template used by your organization. Customize the list of issues by adding, deleting, or changing items as necessary for your specific project. Include the problems documented in the **lessons learned** from your recently completed projects. Ensure that key issues likely to create trouble are listed.

Infrastructure Decisions List

PROJECT PLAN DEVELOPMENT

Overall planning

➤ What life cycle will the plan follow? What project methodology?

➤ Will we be modifying the standard approach? In what way?

➤ What are the major project checkpoints, phase exits, stage gates, or milestones? What deliverables are required for these events?

➤ If there are dependencies on **multiple dependent projects,** how will we identify, document, and agree upon the interfaces?

➤ Where and when will we develop the project plan?

Planning tools

➤ What **software tools for project management** will we use?

➤ Who will use the tool for planning? Tracking?

➤ What training do we require?

Participants

➤ Who in addition to the project leader will be involved in planning?

➤ What are the roles and responsibilities of all participants?

➤ How will remote project contributors participate in planning?

➤ Will the sponsor or other project stakeholders be involved?

Planning deliverables

➤ What are the deliverables of the project planning process?

➤ What is the format for each planning deliverable?

➤ How will we assess the quality of each planning deliverable?

➤ Who will approve planning deliverables?

➤ How will we use the overall project plan for **project baseline setting?**

PROJECT PLAN EXECUTION

Project tracking

➤ How will we do **status collection?** How frequently?

➤ Who will assess project impact using **plan variance analysis?**

➤ What other **project diagnostic metrics** will we track? Who will collect, assess, document, and report their status?

➤ What trends will we track? What are the control limits?

Project reporting

➤ Who will generate **performance reporting?** How frequently?

➤ Who is responsible for **information distribution?**

➤ Who will get project status reports? How?

➤ What reporting is needed for project stakeholders? How often?

➤ How will we communicate issues, problems, and risks?

➤ What criteria will trigger exception reports? Who will receive them?

Project meetings

➤ Where will **meetings** be held? How will **virtual team** members take part?

➤ What types of meetings will we hold? How frequently?

- ➤ Who will produce an agenda for each meeting?
- ➤ Who will keep meeting minutes and distribute them after the meeting?

Project management information system (PMIS)

- ➤ Who will set up the PMIS? What information will it contain?
- ➤ Where will the PMIS be stored? (on-line? WWW? file?)
- ➤ Who will maintain and have change access to the PMIS?
- ➤ Who will have read-only access to the PMIS?
- ➤ For how long will the PMIS be archived after project completion?

INTEGRATED CHANGE CONTROL

Managing project changes

- ➤ When will the plan baseline be frozen? Who approves the freeze?
- ➤ What change control processes will we use?
- ➤ How will we log and track proposed changes?
- ➤ How will we assess the impact of changes?
- ➤ Who will have change approval authority?
- ➤ How will we document and implement accepted project changes?
- ➤ How much deviation from the plan will we accept before initiating a new project baseline derived from a modified project objective?

Continuous improvement and project reviews

- ➤ When will we conduct **project reviews?** Who will participate?
- ➤ What will be reviewed? What processes will we use?
- ➤ How will we document the project review result? Who will receive it?
- ➤ Who will add the data to the project PMIS?

Issue and problem management

- ➤ What process will we use for **decision making?**
- ➤ How will issues and problems be logged and tracked?
- ➤ Who will communicate issue status?
- ➤ What process will we use for **conflict resolution?**
- ➤ What criteria will be used for **problem escalation?**
- ➤ Who has final authority to resolve project disagreements?

Resolve Issues and Document Decisions

Review your list of infrastructure decisions. Eliminate any questions that seem unnecessary and distribute the list to your team.

Solicit recommendations, either in writing or at a meeting. Convene a team meeting to discuss the recommendations and *reach agreement* on each issue.

Document your decisions and your key assumptions. Distribute a summary of the decisions to team members and other stakeholders. Use the decisions in managing your project.

Update the infrastructure as necessary following project changes and during project reviews.

54 **Project Initiation** (PMBOK® 5.1)

WHAT: Obtaining formal commitment to begin a project.

WHEN: Project initiation.

RESULTS: Clear documentation of the project objective and naming of the project leader and initial staff.

Select the Project

Identify why the project is being considered. Projects originate from a wide spectrum of sources:

➤ To solve a current problem

➤ To respond to a stated request

➤ To meet (or create) a market demand

➤ To comply with shifting legal requirements or standards

➤ To improve a process or lower costs

➤ To exploit a technical advance or perform basic research

➤ To pursue a business strategy or opportunity

Define the expected value of the project overall and describe why the project will make a difference, beginning with the process of setting a **project vision.**

Create a rough estimate of both the project benefits and costs. Draft a preliminary scope statement describing the project deliverables. For each defined deliverable, determine the timing required and document the anticipated value represented. Document known project constraints, and make a rough appraisal of likely staffing and other project costs. Summarize the scope, schedule, and resource information in a preliminary **project objective** statement.

Consider the results of (or initiate) a high-level feasibility analysis to validate that the project deliverables are realistic. Assess the project overall, contrasting the cost and value estimates using **return on investment analysis** (ROI) or some other business evaluation technique. Document any important project assumptions. Determine whether to initiate a project through **decision making** based on the best available preliminary information.

Document the Project

Draft the initial **project charter,** collecting:

- The overall business case for the project
- **User needs assessment**
- High-level descriptions of project deliverables, with timing and cost goals
- Any relevant constraints and assumptions
- Information about **sponsorship of the project** and important stakeholders

Commit Initial Resources

Secure funding, equipment, and other resources, at least for **scope planning** and investigation. Identify the project leader and initial core team members, and formally assign them to the project. To get the project off to a robust start, schedule and hold a project **start-up workshop.**

55 Project Metrics – Diagnostic

WHAT: Using ongoing measurements throughout a project to promptly detect adverse variances and trends.

WHEN: Project execution and control.

RESULTS: Early visibility of project problems while they are still small.

Analysis Issues

Diagnostic project metrics are central to **project plan execution. Status collection** is the *source* of most data. For diagnostic metrics, investigate:

➤ Are the data reliable?

➤ Is measurement **variance analysis** due to chronic or one-time factors?

➤ What project improvement options arise from positive variances?

➤ What are the consequences of negative variances?

Example Metrics

Throughout a project, data for understanding the *overall health* of the project is all around you.

Diagnostic *schedule* metrics include:

➤ Critical path activity slippage

➤ Cumulative project slippage

➤ Number of added activities

➤ Early activity completions

➤ Activity closure index: the ratio of activities closed in the project so far to the number expected

Some diagnostic *resource* metrics are:

➤ All **earned value measurement** metrics

➤ Excess consumption of effort or funds

➤ Amount of unplanned overtime

Diagnostic *scope* metrics concern the project deliverable. Consider:

➤ Results of tests, inspections, and walkthroughs

➤ Number and magnitude of approved scope changes

Other diagnostic metrics worth keeping track of include:

➤ Risks added after **project baseline setting**

➤ Issues opened and closed

➤ Communication metrics, such as volumes of e-mail and voicemail

➤ The number of ad hoc project meetings

➤ Impact on other projects

56 **Project Metrics – Predictive**

WHAT: Using bottom-up planning data to forecast project parameters and performance.

WHEN: Project planning, execution and control.

RESULTS: Realistic, plan-based expectations for project performance and data for project communication, negotiations, and decision making.

Predictive Metric Baselines

Baselines for predictive metrics are set using goals from **project initiation** and using *retrospective information* from earlier projects. Predictive project metrics are based on **project plan development.**

Example Predictive Metrics

Predictive metrics are useful for developing a *deeper understanding* of the work and for comparing projects.

Predictive *schedule* metrics include:

➤ **Activity duration estimates**

➤ Project duration (calendar time)

➤ Aggregated schedule risk, schedule reserve

➤ Logical length (maximum number of activities, all paths)

➤ Logical width (maximum number of parallel paths)

➤ Logical project complexity (the ratio of activity dependencies to activities)

➤ Project independence (ratio of internal dependencies to all dependencies)

➤ Sum of all activity durations (if executed sequentially)

➤ Sum of total project activity float

To assess project investment, identify predictive *resource* metrics, such as:

➤ **Cost estimates**

➤ Budget at completion

➤ Total expected project effort

➤ Maximum staff size

➤ Aggregated resource risk, budget reserve

Predictive *scope* metrics can be useful in developing estimates:

➤ Project complexity (interfaces, algorithmic assessments, technical analysis)

➤ Size-based deliverable analysis (component counts, number of major deliverables, lines of noncommented code, blocks on system diagrams)

➤ Volume of anticipated changes

Some *other* predictive metrics for projects include:

➤ **Return on investment analysis** and financial forecasts

➤ **Quantitative risk assessments**

➤ Number of identified risks

57 Project Metrics – Retrospective

WHAT: Using measurements to assess a process after its completion.

WHEN: Project control and closure.

RESULTS: Longer-term process improvement, visibility of trends, and a basis for rewards and recognition.

Retrospective Metric Baselines

Baselines for retrospective metrics are generally set using prior project history and trend assessments. Retrospective metrics are backward looking and may be assessed only at the close of a project. These metrics are most useful for longer-term **process improvement.**

Example Metrics

Retrospective metrics help project leaders assess whether the project was *effectively managed* and may be used to calibrate processes for generating predictive metrics.

A few retrospective *schedule* metrics are:

➤ Actual durations compared to planned schedule

➤ Number of new unplanned activities

➤ Assessment of estimation accuracy

➤ Performance to standard estimates for standardized project activities

Retrospective *resource* metrics include:

➤ Actual budget compared to planned budget

➤ Total project effort

➤ Life-cycle phase effort percentages

➤ Late project defect correction effort as a percentage of total effort

➤ Added staff

➤ Staff turnover

➤ Variances in travel, communications, equipment, outsourcing, or other expense subcategories

Retrospective *scope* metrics relate to your development processes:

➤ Actual "size" of project deliverable analysis (components, lines of non-commented code, system interfaces)

➤ Number of accepted changes

➤ Number of defects

➤ Performance of deliverables compared to **project objectives**

Other retrospective metrics worth considering are:

➤ Number of project risks encountered

➤ Project issues tracked and closed

58 Project Metrics – Selecting and Implementing

WHAT: Defining and using a set of project measures.

WHEN: Project planning, execution, and control.

RESULTS: Encouragement of desired behaviors, objective baselines for measuring progress and performance, and timely triggers for process improvement.

Document Desired Behaviors and Outcomes

Before deciding what to measure on projects, define the behaviors you seek. Measurement affects behavior, so clearly define *desired results* and use them to guide selection of metrics.

Metrics are of three basic types: *predictive, diagnostic, and retrospective.* Useful systems of metrics will generally include a good balance of measurement types.

➤ **Project predictive metrics** use analysis to provide forecasts of future conditions. Most predictive project metrics are based on **project plan development** outputs, such as **quantitative risk management** assessments, **activity duration estimates,** and **cost estimates.**

➤ **Project diagnostic metrics** provide current data on **project plan execution.** Based on **status collection,** they are used for **plan variance analysis** and **performance reporting.** Diagnostic project metrics include the measurements of **earned value management.**

➤ **Project retrospective metrics** report on process performance and health following completion. Some retrospective metrics are used to validate predictive metrics. Retrospective measures are integral to **lessons learned,** and for the overall project they are part of **administrative closure.**

Define a Set of Measures

A project is a complex system, so one metric will generally not be sufficient. Too many metrics are also undesirable; important information will be lost in the jumble. Strive to define a *minimum set* of project metrics to give a balanced project view.

Select metrics for:

➤ *Objectivity:* If metrics are evaluated by different people, all will get the same result.

> *Accessibility:* Good metrics are easy to collect.

> *Clarity:* Verify through discussion that everyone understands the measurement process and uses consistent units of measure.

> *Frequency:* Collect data frequently enough to support the results you desire, but not so often that it represents unduly high overhead.

> *Importance:* Collect only metrics that will make a meaningful difference; do not collect data just because you can.

> *Tension:* Metrics assessing speed and accuracy used alone may cause undesirable behavior, but together their tension results in desired performance.

> *No gaming:* Eliminate factors that can improve the measurement without achieving desired results.

Define and document each project metric clearly to minimize differing interpretations in a *metric data sheet.* Include information such as: the name of the metric, the intended objective, required data, measurement units, frequency, collection method, any formulas used, the target acceptable range, who will make the measurement, and how it will be achieved.

Establish a Measurement Baseline

Before using the metrics, collect data to define a *normal range.* For new diagnostic metrics, you can begin with an educated guess, but confirm the baseline using the first several cycles of data collection. For retrospective metrics, set baselines using existing data from earlier projects. For predictive metrics, verify baselines using corresponding retrospective metrics (for example, validate financial ROI predictions against actual returns).

Use the System of Metrics

Metrics drive behavior, so selecting appropriate factors to measure can have a significant effect on **motivation** and project progress. Hewlett-Packard founder Bill Hewlett was fond of saying, *"What gets measured gets done."*

Collect project data to support project **decision making** and **process improvement.** Project metrics also provide the historical basis for **activity duration estimates, cost estimates, resource planning,** and project control. Following changes, review the measurement baseline and acceptable range for each metric.

Throughout the project, make the measurements *visible*. Report the status of metrics to all project stakeholders who need or are affected by the measurements.

Finally, work to ensure that any metrics collected are used primarily for process monitoring and improvement, *not for punishment*. Metrics used to rank people or for **canceling projects** are unreliable and will be gamed.

59 Project Objective (Mission)

WHAT: A brief, high-level description of the desired project deliverable, timing, and investment.

WHEN: Project initiation and planning.

RESULTS: A clear, unambiguous statement of what is expected of the project, validated by its sponsor.

Draft the Project Objective

The initial project objective should be based on **project initiation** data. A project objective is a *simple, short statement* describing the project. It is generally composed by the project leader, often with inputs from the project team, but it can also be written by the project sponsor, a customer, or other project stakeholders.

A project objective defines the deliverable(s) (*scope*), the deadline (*schedule*), and the overall investment (*cost*). A good objective is about twenty-five words in length and captures project essentials concisely. It should avoid technical jargon, acronyms, idioms, or other language that can lead to misunderstandings. Describe deliverables using ordinary language that all project stakeholders will understand. Translate the information into any languages necessary, and validate the translations before distribution. For timing, include the day, month (by name, not number), and year. Specify resources in clear monetary terms or in unambiguous effort.

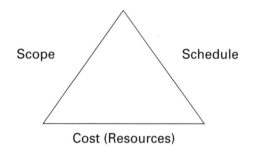

Scope   Schedule

Cost (Resources)

An example: "I believe this nation should commit itself to achieving the goal, before this decade is out, of landing a man on the moon and returning him safely to earth . . . $531 million in this fiscal year." (President John F. Kennedy, 1961)

Validate the Project Objective

Validate the project objective with the project sponsor before continuing with **scope planning** and other projects. Show the objective statement to the sponsor and other stakeholders to probe for potential misunderstandings about the project. Work to clarify the details and to test interpretations, so you can correct any omissions or errors prior to detailed project definition and planning. The project objective is merely a restatement of the initial top-down goal, not a firm commitment, so ensure that the result of this validation is only a *mutual agreement on the project goals.*

Document and Use the Project Objective

Discuss the project objective with the project team, and document it as part of the **project charter.** Add the objective to project documents and use it in project meetings and communications.

Use the project objective to set **project priorities,** to establish the **project vision,** to define the **project infrastructure,** and as the basis for **project plan development.** Make the project objective central to **decision making, scope change control,** and **project reviews.**

60 Project Office

WHAT: Using specialized staff to consolidate many project management responsibilities for a group of related projects.

WHEN: Throughout large projects.

RESULTS: Consistent processes and reporting for related projects, minimized overhead, and increased likelihood of success.

Justify

A competent and well-staffed project office (also called a program management office, a project management center of excellence, a project support team, and many similar names) brings many *benefits*, such as:

➤ Use of high-end **software tools for project management** while avoiding excess investment in training and tool deployment through centralization

➤ Improved cross-project resource planning and management

➤ Better support for distributed and global projects

➤ Avoidance of the "too many projects" problem through coherent portfolio management

Functions performed by staff members of a project office include:

➤ Facilitating project **start-up workshops**

➤ Support for **project plan development** and **communications planning**

➤ Consistent and efficient creation of project planning documents

➤ Enforcement of planning standards and auditing for completeness

➤ Centralization of **status collection, information distribution, performance reporting,** and **integrated change control**

➤ Assistance with **plan variance analysis** and recommendations for resolution

➤ Collection and analysis of **project metrics** during **project plan execution**

➤ Assistance with **conflict resolution, decision-making,** management of timing, specification, resource, staffing, and other project issues, and facilitation of **problem escalation**

➤ Planning, execution, and reporting for **project reviews, administrative closure,** and **lessons learned**

A project office also has *costs,* for staffing, communication, set up, training, equipment, and related expenses.

Before **organizing for project management** by establishing a project office, determine what functions and specialties are worth implementing. Carefully consider the *net value* of creating a dedicated project support team.

Implement

Identify the functions that will be centralized in the project office, and estimate the staffing that will be required. Use **required skills analysis** to determine what the staff members need to know, and work to *build the skills* through training, hiring, or other strategies. At a minimum, project office staffing should be adept at:

➤ Planning

➤ Project communication support

➤ **Information distribution** and **performance reporting**

➤ **Coaching and mentoring** for project leaders

➤ Management of **organizational change**

61 **Project Plan Development** (PMBOK® 4.1)

WHAT: Developing a detailed, bottom-up description of the project work.

WHEN: Project planning, execution, and control.

RESULTS: A basis for effective communication and a map for project success.

Prepare for Planning

Like a chess player, a good project manager plans several moves ahead. This process is an *overall summary* of many other processes described throughout this book. A summary flowchart indicates how some of the planning processes are linked, but project planning is iterative, and so there are many other possibilities.

Prepare for planning by reviewing **project initiation** information, the **project objective,** and other available documentation such as the **project charter.** Document and use **project infrastructure** planning decisions to guide your efforts.

Involve the core team in planning, as well as any others you need to model and document the overall project plans effectively.

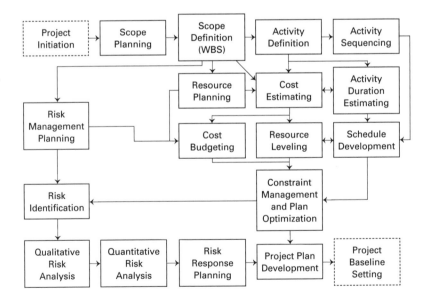

Develop the Plans

At the start of planning, information about *expected deliverables* is often the clearest, so **scope planning** and **scope definition** are generally where planning begins. The work breakdown structure (WBS) from scope definition serves as the bottom-up foundation for all other planning, including **risk management planning.**

Activity definition (derived from the WBS) supports *preliminary scheduling*, which is usually next. **Activity duration estimating** and **activity sequencing** for each defined activity provide the information needed for workflow analysis. Done in parallel, their outputs feed into **schedule development**, often facilitated by **software tools for project management.** Using the preliminary schedule, you can create Gantt charts, activity networks, a critical path analysis, and other time-based deliverables.

As the timeline for the project takes shape, the focus of planning shifts to determining *resources and staffing.* **Resource planning** uses the WBS to do **required skills analysis** and **responsibility analysis,** and to support **staff acquisition.** Activity definitions and data from the WBS are also used for effort analysis and **cost estimation.** Reconciling the cost (based on effort) and duration (based on availability) estimates leads to a resource-loaded refinement of the preliminary schedule and permits **resource leveling** analysis. Cost estimates, other resource data, and your risk planning can then be aggregated for initial **cost budgeting.**

Unfortunately, the results of the initial bottom-up analysis rarely are consistent with the project's top-down objective, so *replanning* and "what if?" analysis using the techniques of **constraint management and plan optimization** are needed. Use **project priorities** to explore trade-offs in your preliminary plan. If you are unsuccessful in creating a satisfactory plan through replanning, develop several alternative project plans that are as close to the stated goals as possible.

The final part of plan development, because it relies on all other planning data, is *risk management.* **Risk identification** is a good idea throughout planning, as your analysis can reveal uncertainty, lack of enthusiasm, potential failure modes, and other detrimental factors. As initial planning approaches completion, **brainstorm** and list additional risks. **Qualitative risk analysis** prioritizes identified risks, guiding risk management decisions. **Quantitative risk analysis** may be done to assess significant risks, supporting your **risk response planning.** Integrate any risk prevention tactics into your plans, and document any contingency plans you create.

Plan development culminates in inspecting the plan for any defects, correcting them, and *documenting all planning deliverables* in the appropriate format.

Finalize Your Plans

If your best plan fails to support the top-down objective, use plan alternatives to **negotiate project changes.** *Validate the plan* with your sponsor and complete **project baseline setting.**

62 **Project Plan Execution** (PMBOK® 4.2)

WHAT: Executing and controlling a project, using the baseline plan.

WHEN: Project execution and control.

RESULTS: Early detection of issues and problems, accurate and timely progress reporting, and effective project communications.

Prepare

This process is an *overall summary* of many other processes described throughout this book. A summary flowchart indicates some process dependencies.

Project tracking and control processes commence with **project baseline setting.** Once deliverable specifications are frozen and you have a baseline plan, you have a *foundation for project tracking* and control. Review the process for **scope change control** with the project team and begin using it to resist unnecessary changes.

Refine your communication processes to meet the needs of your team, stakeholders, and sponsor. Document your **project infrastructure** execution

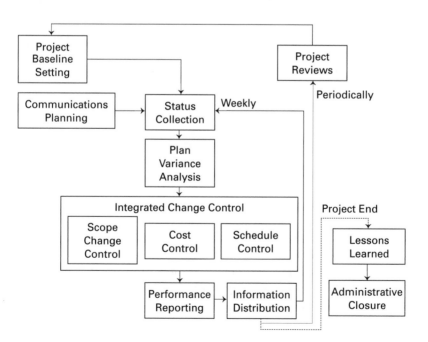

decisions and your **communications plan.** Establish and deliver on expectations for communication, meetings, and reporting.

The Status Cycle

Project monitoring depends on a *four-stage cycle* that repeats (weekly for most projects) until the end of the project.

The first stage is *inbound communication,* **status collection** by the project leader.

The second stage of the cycle includes comparison of status data to the baseline plan and **plan variance analysis.** The *data analysis* also involves evaluation of **project diagnostic metrics,** including those used for **earned value management.**

The third stage is for *project control,* responding to any timing or resource problems using the processes of **integrated change control,** principally **cost control, schedule control,** and **scope change control.** When project variances are beyond your ability to remedy, promptly seek help from those with more authority through **problem escalation.**

The fourth and final stage is *outbound communication,* to inform people of what has happened on the project. Examples include **performance reporting, information distribution,** and any project **presentations.** These follow the analysis and planning of the prior stages, so that you can include credible plans for recovery along with any bad news you need to deliver.

At the end of each cycle, *archive* all status, change, and other project reporting in the project management information system.

Review

For projects longer than six months in duration, conduct periodic **project reviews** to *revalidate the project plans* and collect new information. When necessary, **negotiate project changes** and validate a new project baseline to reflect current reality.

Closure

When the *project is completed,* get formal acceptance of your deliverable through **scope verification** and prepare a final status report to inform everyone that the project is over. Complete **administrative closure** by analyzing the **lessons learned** on the project and document your recommendations.

Thank all the team members for their contributions, and use programs for **rewards and recognition** when appropriate to recognize significant accomplishments. *Celebrate your successes.*

63 **Project Priorities**

WHAT: Explicitly identifying decision criteria for the project.

WHEN: Project planning and control.

RESULTS: Effective management of project changes and prompt, consistent decisions.

Objectives and Constraints

Review the **project objective** and the assumptions and constraints identified during **project initiation.** Explore the reasons for the goals and constraints, and document the *consequences* of failing to achieve them. If necessary, probe for more information on constraints and goals with the project sponsor and key stakeholders.

Set the Priorities

For most projects, all three parameters—scope, schedule, and cost (resources) —are important. Setting priorities enables the project team to determine which of the three is most *essential.* These priorities support **scope planning, decision making, constraint management and plan optimization, negotiating project changes,** and **integrated change control.**

Consider the *trade-offs* between scope, schedule, and cost by specifying small changes to the stated project objective. Would it be worse to slip the schedule a week beyond the deadline, or increase the project budget by 5 percent? Would it be more appropriate to drop a feature of a project deliverable or to add staff to the project team? Would a slightly longer project that delivers a more robust product be desirable? Questions such as these often arise late in a project, but it is better to deal with them early.

In exploring the costs, pain, and appropriateness of small changes, relative priorities emerge. Document priorities using a *three-by-three matrix.* Place one mark in each row, showing which parameter is constrained (least flexible), which one is to be optimized (somewhat flexible), and for which of the three change may be accepted (most flexible).

Consider the options (there are six), and discuss them within the project team to develop *consensus* on the priorities.

Validate your prioritization with your project sponsors and stakeholders, and make modifications if needed based on their feedback. For some projects, agreeing to constrain two of the three parameters may be necessary, but

	Schedule	Scope	Cost
Constrained Least Flexible	●		
Optimized Somewhat Flexible			●
Accepted Most Flexible		●	

it is always unrealistic to limit all three, especially prior to **project plan development.** Strive for agreement, and clearly document the lowest priority.

Periodically Review Priorities

Keep the matrix *up to date.* If your project changes, reevaluate the priorities to ensure they remain appropriate. Revisit the priorities following business reorganizations and during **project reviews.** If the priorities shift, revalidate them and update the project documentation.

64 **Project Review**

WHAT: Periodically revisiting project plans, assumptions, and constraints during long projects.

WHEN: Project execution and control.

RESULTS: Revalidation of project objectives, improved project plans, and renewal of team motivation.

Plan and Schedule Periodic Reviews

Projects are all unique, so planning more than a few months in advance with precision is difficult. Depending on the project type, reviews aligned with the *planning horizon,* every three to six months, allow necessary **project plan development** adjustments.

Weekly **status collection, performance reporting,** and **integrated change control** are all necessary, but on longer projects they are not sufficient. Periodic reviews provide the project equivalent of planned *preventative maintenance.*

Project reviews are most useful at natural *project transitions:*

➤ Life-cycle or phase transitions

➤ Major milestones or checkpoints

➤ Following significant project changes

➤ When new members are either added to or leaving project staff

➤ After business reorganizations

➤ At the end of a fiscal quarter

Plan the review in advance, allowing sufficient time (several hours, minimum) to cover the items on your agenda, such as:

➤ Recognition of significant accomplishments

➤ Reinforcement of **teamwork** and relationships

➤ Review of the **project objective**

➤ Revalidation of project constraints and assumptions

➤ New **activity definition** and **risk identification**

➤ Revisions to **activity duration estimating** and **activity sequencing**

➤ Review of **resource planning** and **cost estimating**

- ➤ Review **contract administration**
- ➤ Adjustments to **project infrastructure**
- ➤ Analysis of project trends and changes
- ➤ Collection of **lessons learned** and opportunities for **process improvement**

Determine the *team members* who need to attend, and choose a time when they are available. Get their commitment to attend in person whenever possible.

Assemble *needed information* from the project archive, and update any information such as **market research** or **customer interviews** that might be out of date.

Review the Project

Begin the project review by discussing the agenda. Discuss lessons learned, starting with things that went well and major accomplishments.

Focus the remainder of the review on new information and on potential *project changes.* Review the future project plans, and test the assumptions, estimates, and other information in your project plans using what you now know.

During the review, *capture decisions and action items* in writing, and maintain a separate list of any project issues that require later attention but are beyond the scope of the review meeting.

At the close of the review, discuss all the recommendations, suggestions, and decisions, and assign owners and due dates for all added project activities and action items. Set a date for updating any project documents affected by the review.

Implement Recommendations and Follow Up

Document the review. Summarize the meeting and distribute a report, generally to the same people who receive your project status reports. Replace any project plans and documents that are updated, and archive all older versions, marking them as obsolete.

Implement recommendations that you have authority to make. For project changes, use your change control process, and make approved changes as soon as practical. If major changes are needed, use your data to **negotiate project changes** and for revised **project baseline setting.**

After the review, prepare a **presentation** to summarize the project's progress to date, and your plans going forward. Invite stakeholders and people from related projects to attend. Accentuate the positive, and *use the presentation* to enhance project team **motivation.**

Also use project reviews as an opportumity for **rewards and recognition.** *Thank people* personally for their contributions, and consider scheduling an event for the project team to recognize accomplishments. Long projects, especially, need more parties.

65 **Project Vision**

WHAT: A clear and motivating statement of why the project matters.

WHEN: Project initiation and planning.

RESULTS: Sustained team enthusiasm for the project.

Assess the Current Environment

Review the status quo. *Collect information* about:

➤ **Sponsorship of the project**

➤ The project basis from **project initiation**

➤ The **project objective**

➤ The history and any specific problems preceding the project

➤ Trends and **user needs assessment**

➤ Overall business strategies and stakeholder opinions

➤ Organizational values

➤ Project team values

Draft the Project Vision Statement

Gather project team members to craft a vision statement. For some projects, a vision statement may not be needed, but a well-worded description of a desired future state provides a good foundation for **teamwork** and group **motivation.** Building a shared vision strengthens relationships and trust.

Discuss the *improved future* following successful completion of your project (or, if your project is a part of a larger program, after completion of the overall effort). Think about the future for yourselves, your organization, users or customers, and your project stakeholders.

Develop a *vivid description* of the resulting future, capturing the benefits and stating why they are important to you and to others. Emphasize how the project contributes to the desired future, and use clear, engaging, and emotional words to convey a strong image.

Keep the end in mind. Describe why you want to get there, in *qualitative* terms. Metrics are necessary for individual goals and project objectives, but visions are more inspirational. Effective visions are short, simple, and easy to remember.

Test each proposed vision statement within the team.

➤ Is it consistent with the values of the project team?

➤ Does it pass the "What's in it for me?" test?

➤ Is the vision challenging, and one the team can take pride in sharing?

➤ Is it sufficiently realistic to be motivational?

➤ Is it memorable?

An example vision: "[We will create] a motor car for the great multitude. It will be so low in price that no man making a good salary will be unable to own one. The automobile will be taken for granted ... [and we will] give a large number of men employment at good wages." (Henry Ford)

Pursue the Project Vision

Document the project vision, and make it part of **meetings, presentations, project reviews,** and reporting. Keep the vision visible using signs, websites, and other methods.

Frequently *remind* team members and stakeholders of the vision, and use it in **informal communications.** Show enthusiasm for the vision and reinforce it until people see it as inevitable. Projects do not succeed because they are easy; they succeed because people care about them.

Use the vision to overcome barriers, to manage change, and to support **decision making.** Align **rewards and recognition** with the vision.

66 **Qualitative Risk Analysis** (PMBOK® 11.3)

WHAT: Assessing and prioritizing known project risks.

WHEN: Project planning, execution, and control.

RESULTS: Identification of the most severe project risks, based on relative probability and project impact.

Risk Assessment

Risk analysis involves using the processes defined in the **project risk management planning** on each of the risks listed as a result of **risk identification.** All assessment of risk depends on determining *risk probability and risk impact.* Qualitative analysis combines range estimates of these two factors to prioritize project risks. **Quantitative risk analysis** depends on numerical estimates to determine the precise consequences of project risks.

Probability Ranges

The likelihood or probability for a risk event must always be between zero and one. Qualitative risk assessment depends on defined *probability ranges* between these limits, using defined percentages.

Projects may use two, three, or more ranges for assessment, trading off between fewer (to simplify the process) or more (to improve precision). *Three ranges* offer a reasonable balance between obtaining team agreement and ability to sort potential risks by severity. Risk assessment using this method uses ranges of high, moderate, and low, often defined as:

➤ High: 50 percent or higher probability

➤ Moderate: Between 10 and 50 percent probability

➤ Low: Less than 10 percent probability

Additional probability ranges may be defined, with associated percentages suitable for your projects.

Impact Ranges

Risk impact can be difficult to define as it has many dimensions. Impact may be measured in many different ways, such as time, cost, effort, scope change, team confidence, and customer trust. As with probability, the minimum is zero, but the maximum value is specific to the risk. *Impact ranges* for qualitative

Risks	Probability (H/M/L)	Impact (H/M/L)	Overall Risk
Expert Is Busy	M	H	HM
Component Late	M	M	M
Test Gear Unavailable	L	L	L

Risk Assessment Table

risk assessment generally rely on categories defined by the magnitude of risk consequences.

Although any number of impact categories may be defined, for most projects adequate qualitative analysis can be done using *three ranges,* typically defined as:

➤ High: Project objectives must be changed (scope, schedule, or resource).

➤ Moderate: Project objectives are safe, but replanning is necessary.

➤ Low: No significant changes to objectives or plans are needed.

Assessment

Risk assessment tables begin with the risk register list and determine overall risk for each potential problem by combining the probability and impact assessments. This may be done by simply combining the range categories, or by assigning numeric values to the categories (such as 9, 3, and 1 for High, Moderate, and Low) and multiplying the factors together.

A similar qualitative assessment method uses a *risk assessment matrix* to place risks in a two-dimensional grid. Categories of probability and impact define where in the matrix each potential exposure falls, with the most severe toward the top and the right. Again, any number of categories may be used, defined as appropriate for your project, and risk assessment matrices do not need to be square.

Risk Prioritization

Use qualitative risk assessment to *rank order* the risks identified in your risk register, listing the most serious potential problems at the top and the more

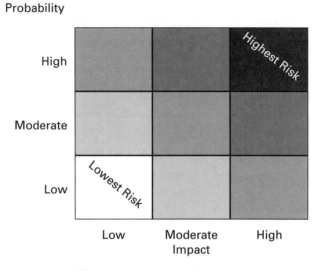

Probability

High

Moderate

Low

Highest Risk

Lowest Risk

Low   Moderate   High
Impact

Risk Assessment Matrix

trivial risks at the bottom. Identify severe risks for quantitative analysis and **risk response planning.**

Use the sorted list to determine *overall project risk* and to increase the visibility of the potential consequences of the most significant risks.

67 **Quality Assurance** (PMBOK® 8.2)

WHAT: Routine tracking of project output against quantified objectives.

WHEN: Project execution and control.

RESULTS: Prompt detection of process issues and revision of work methods.

Quality assurance serves two primary purposes on projects. It detects processes that are in need of revision, so they can be improved. It also enforces established standards for work being done using improper methods.

Audit

Maintaining project quality requires periodic *process re-examination.* Some process audits are scheduled as part of **quality planning.** Other audits are triggered by **plan variance analysis, quality control** problems, **project reviews,** or **lessons learned.**

Whatever the motivation, quality assurance begins with a list of all known problems related to project processes, and probes to detect any additional issues. If any measured results are not as planned (both adverse variances and beneficial ones), there may be a process problem. Examine the cost and effort required to do project work to detect examples of situations where the outputs may be acceptable but the execution efficiency is poor. Interview team members involved in project activities to discover processes that are ineffective or unsuitable for the work. *List all issues* for analysis.

Analyze

Initially, check that the measurements are valid and that the work is being done using the appropriate process. If you detect that measurement inaccuracy or alternative work methods are causing problems, confront the situation. Discuss it with the individuals involved, and get their commitment for accuracy and *compliance.*

For other issues, use **cause-and-effect analysis** to detect *root causes.* Work with the project team and appropriate stakeholders to find options for **process improvement.**

If the problems impact project scope and seem irresolvable, prepare to **negotiate project changes** and use **scope change control** to manage any specification changes. Resolving process problems that arise from organizational dependencies may require changes that are beyond the authority of your project team. "**Influence without authority**" techniques can be effective, but you may ultimately need to try **problem escalation.** Through your analysis, determine necessary process and other changes and document the situation and your *proposed response.*

Implement and Track

Get any necessary *approval* for process changes, using project **integrated change control.** Document all new processes, and communicate the reasons for **organizational change** to all the people affected.

Implement your recommended process changes.

Monitor the new process for expected results. If results are inadequate, or there are unintended problematic consequences, initiate further analysis.

68 Quality Control (PMBOK® 8.3)

WHAT: Ongoing monitoring of project work compared with plans and standards.

WHEN: Throughout a project.

RESULTS: Prompt recognition of quality problems and effective project control.

Data Collection

Project quality control depends on the *quality management plan* from **quality planning.** Expected measurements and methods for achieving them are part of the project baseline plan.

Project **status collection** and *project deliverable data* from testing, checklists, and inspections provide the information needed to detect variations between the results expected and the results produced.

Data Analysis

The field of statistics provides many *techniques* for detecting problems in deliverable quality and defects in development processes. Among these are:

➤ Scatter diagrams

➤ Histograms and sampling distributions

➤ Trend and control limit analysis

➤ Pareto charts

These techniques can differentiate normal project execution from problem situations, such as results that:

➤ Are outside an acceptable range

➤ Display excessive variability

➤ Change in suspicious, non-random ways

➤ Display disturbing trends

Plan

Examining the situation using **cause-and-effect analysis,** interviews, discussions, inspections, and observations will generally reveal the *problem source.*

Depending on the source, find an *appropriate response.* **Performance problem resolution** is necessary if the individuals doing the work are at fault.

If the inputs to a process are faulty, resolution will require better monitoring and control of those dependencies. Other situations may require recalibration, replacement, or repair of equipment used in the development process. If the process itself is suspected to be the problem, a process audit as part of ongoing **quality assurance** or a **process improvement** project might be the answer.

Select the most promising approach and document it.

Do

If necessary, obtain approval for any changes through **integrated change control.** *Implement* the approach you selected for resolving the quality problem.

Check

Monitor **project diagnostic metrics** to verify the outcomes you expect and to detect any unintended adverse consequences.

Act

If there are remaining problems or newly created ones, initiate a *new quality control cycle*. Back out any changes that resulted in outputs that are worse than the original situation.

If the changes are effective, *update* the project plans, process documentation, and other materials affected.

Communicate all changes made to affected individuals, and incorporate the results of your efforts in project **performance reporting.**

69 Quality Planning (PMBOK® 8.1)

WHAT: Defining measurable standards for project results and determining how to achieve them.

WHEN: Project planning.

RESULTS: Quantified project standards and objectives, supported by explicit plans.

Quality management for projects borrows heavily from methodologies primarily associated with production and manufacturing such as Total Quality Management (TQM). The primary goal of project quality management is defining and delivering *realistic project deliverables,* so it is closely related to scope management.

Determine Customer Requirements

Use techniques such as **customer interviews, market research,** and product benchmarking to complete a thorough **user needs assessment.** Probe to *quantify the value* of the needs, and state why they matter, using the "voice of the customer."

Determine the cost of achieving the requirements through **cost estimating** and **project plan development,** and use *cost–benefit analysis* to decide which requirements are appropriate for the project. Prioritize the list of requirements and use the top items to set specifications for the project deliverable.

Document Specifications

Review organizational quality policies, requirements, and standards (for example, programs such as ISO 9000 or Six Sigma), and use them in **project scope planning** to integrate the accepted specifications into the final *project scope statement.*

Quantify each specification, and develop any acceptance tests that will be required for **scope verification.** Define the *final approval criteria* for project results at the project start, and get sign-off for acceptance tests from appropriate stakeholders and customers during project planning. If necessary, seek assistance of statistical experts in the design of experiments and development of your tests.

Establish Plans

Review your development processes for defects or potential problems. Use **process improvement** and mapping techniques to determine opportunities; quality is planned in, not inspected in.

Add all quality-related activities, such as process audits, tests, and approvals, into the project *work breakdown structure* during **scope definition.** If there is significant cost or effort involved, seek and obtain appropriate approval. Document your quality plans, either separately or as part of the overall project plan. Develop any needed checklists, guidelines, and process documentation you will require.

Determine the *people* who have responsibility for project **quality assurance** (process assessment) and **quality control** (results assessment), and get their commitment for the work. If your project will require participation from quality specialists, discuss your project with them to ensure that they understand and approve of your overall plans.

70 **Quantitative Risk Analysis** (PMBOK® 11.4)

WHAT: Assessing risk severity in numerical terms.

WHEN: Project planning, execution, and control.

RESULTS: Risk impact assessments in absolute units, such as time, cost, or effort.

Quantitative Assessment

Quantitative risk analysis applies processes defined in the **project risk management planning** on risks determined using **risk identification.** Generally **qualitative risk assessment** is done for all listed risks, to determine which project risks may justify more precise quantitative analysis. Quantitative analysis requires greater effort, but it generates *absolute estimates* of risk probability and impact for the most severe project risks.

Converting Probability Ranges to Estimates

In the place of the ranges used for qualitative risk analysis, quantitative assessment uses a numerical percentage, a specific fraction between 0 and 100 percent. There are *three ways* to estimate probabilities:

➤ A prediction, based on a mathematical model

➤ An empirical calculation using historical data

➤ Selection of a number based on the best analysis available

Some risk situations may be modeled and in other cases there may be sufficient data to use in statistical forecasting. However, because many project risks are unique, complex, and rarely occurring, the third technique (better known as *guessing*) is most frequently used. Quantitative risk probability estimates are often inexact.

Converting Impact Ranges to Estimates

The categories of impact used in qualitative analysis also must be made precise, requiring definition of units (possibly several) and a *numeric estimate* of project impact measured in these units. For some risks, a single estimate will be appropriate, but for others it may be best expressed as a statistical distribution or a histogram. Quantitative risk impact is measured in days of project slip, money, effort, or some other suitable unit. Most risks have impact in more than one of these units, such as both time and cost.

Cost impact is straightforward, using **cost estimating** techniques and measured in dollars, yen, euros, or some other monetary unit. Effort impact, measured in units such as person-days, uses effort estimation methods.

Schedule impact is more difficult. Timing impact analysis requires new **activity duration estimating,** but not every activity duration increase will necessarily change the overall project schedule. Only the slippage in excess of any float determined in **schedule development** represents measurable project impact.

Other impact categories, including staff productivity, scope modifications, and other changes, must also be identified and estimated as precisely as possible, using the techniques of **project plan development.** While the foundations of quantitative risk analysis impact may seem precise, the quality of the estimates is quite variable.

Assessment

Risk assessments using *tables, grids, and matrices* are similar to those used for qualitative risk analysis, substituting the actual probability percentages and numerical estimates of impact for the ranges and categories. Matrices using numerical data are generally replaced by two-dimensional graphs. Because impact may be estimated in cost, schedule, and other possible units, more than one representation may be necessary.

For simple projects, a quick inspection of the plan using the risk assessments will reveal the risks most likely to cause the most damage. For more complex projects, *sensitivity analysis,* done using a copy of the schedule data entered into a **software tool for project management,** is a fast way to identify risks (and combinations of risks) that are most likely to result in project delay. Sequentially entering risk data and then backing it out reveals overall schedule sensitivity, using quantitative "what if?" scenario analysis.

For complex, multi-option project branch points in the plan that are dependent on data not yet available, *decision trees* may be used to assess expected outcomes quantitatively and to develop risk information about a project. Decision-tree analysis may be done for time, cost, or other measurable project parameters.

Quantitative Modeling and Computer Simulation

Using a range of estimates for time (or cost) for Monte Carlo simulation provides the basis of the *Program Evaluation and Review Technique* (PERT). PERT was originally created to assess quantitatively overall project risk, based on three estimates (optimistic, most likely, and pessimistic), defining the mean and variance (risk) for each project estimate. Computer simulation or statistical analysis of the schedule (PERT time) provides an overall assessment of project schedule risk, and similar analysis of cost estimates (PERT cost) determines budget risk.

Document Risks and Specific Estimated Consequences

For significant activity-related risks assessed quantitatively, document measured *risk consequences* in the project risk register. Select significant risks for **risk response planning.**

Aggregate the quantitative risk assessment information to assess *overall project risk*. Calculate **project predictive metrics** to determine aspects of the project that are larger or more complex than those you have managed in the past.

71 Required Skills Analysis

WHAT: Determining the skills required to complete the project.

WHEN: Project planning.

RESULTS: A summary of the skills needed for project work, including experience and proficiency levels.

Review the WBS

Skills analysis is a key portion of **resource planning.** For each **activity definition** from the project work breakdown structure (WBS) developed in **scope definition,** list the owner and any other contributors who are committed to the work. A **responsibility analysis** matrix is one way to summarize *activity staffing* for WBS activities.

Determine the Skills Needed

List the *necessary skills* and background needed to complete each activity, including:

➤ Knowledge in specific areas

➤ Proficiency with tools and equipment

➤ Experience with applications and systems

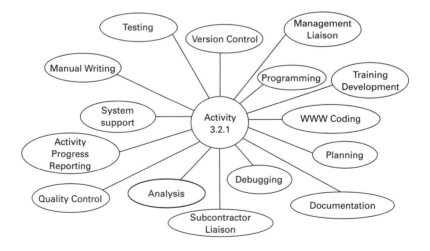

➤ Communication and language abilities

➤ Amount and level of experience in a given field

Drawing a "mind map" for each identified project activity is an effective way to get started.

Identify Gaps and Document Capabilities

List unmet skill needs. Identify all specific skill requirements for which you lack a credible commitment from a capable, named individual.

Also list the *available skills.* Resolve any skill gaps through **staff acquisition,** or seek alternative methods for the work using skills available on the team during **project plan development.**

Staffing a project with only specialists can be risky, as problems will undoubtedly arise that cross functional boundaries or fall outside the fields covered by staff specialists. Include "*generalist*" as a required skill at the project level, and work to include people who are adept at handling unexpected situations.

72 **Resource Leveling**

WHAT: Reconciling project plans with available resources by minimizing overcommitments and identifying underused staff.

WHEN: Project planning.

RESULTS: A bottom-up project resource plan and schedule consistent with committed project resources.

Profile Required Resources

Use **cost estimating** and **schedule development** to develop a resource-loaded schedule. **Software tools for project management** assist in automating this, but *resource histograms* for staffing and other important project resources can be created using spreadsheets, project databases, and other methods.

Identify Deficits and Surpluses

Inspect the analysis from a histogram or spreadsheet. For each project contributor, identify *overcommitments*—periods during the project where his or her planned work exceeds the available capacity. Also note any periods for contributors where the current draft plan indicates that they have potentially available time.

Example of a resource histogram from Microsoft Project:

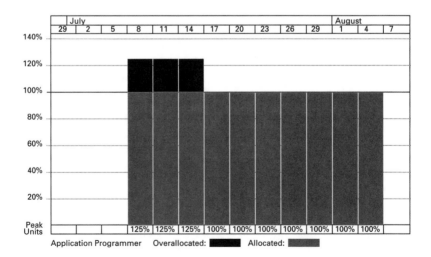

Repeat the analysis for the project as a whole, to identify the places in the preliminary project plan where *overall staffing* is inadequate.

Reconcile Differences

Project management software tools generally have an *automated function* for resource leveling. While the function may sometimes prove useful, always back up the data in your plan before you try it; automated leveling generally makes projects unrecognizable.

Another approach to resource leveling is to identify resource bottlenecks in the plan and make revisions *manually.* Consider modifications to minimize resource conflicts, such as:

➤ Splitting activities into discontinuous work with one or more timing gaps

➤ Changing the planned rate of effort by extending **activity duration estimates**

➤ Shifting planned resource use to conform better to the available pool

➤ Shortening some activity durations using undercommitted project staff

➤ Proposing scope modifications or delays in delivery

➤ Building a case for additional **staff acquisition**

Identify options available for your project using suitable "what if" analysis (a separate copy of a scheduling tool database is a quick and effective way to do this), and *select ideas* that resolve your resource capacity constraints.

Update project plans, schedules, and other planning documents.

73 **Resource Planning** (PMBOK® 7.1)

WHAT: Documenting the people, funding, equipment, and other resources needed for the project.

WHEN: Project planning.

RESULTS: A detailed description of required resources and assignments, based on project plans.

Determine Required Resources

Estimate resources necessary for the project. The process requires both an overall assessment of the amount of each type of resource and specific identification of skills, responsibility, and details.

At the highest level, resource planning uses **cost budgeting** to determine the *total expected cost* of a project by accumulating the **cost estimations** associated with each project **activity definition.**

Use effort estimation (generally the largest component of cost estimation) combined with **schedule development** to develop a *required resource profile.* A time-scaled histogram from a **software tool for project management,** a spreadsheet, or other analysis can be used to determine the amount of project staffing needed for each part of the project.

Using the activities identified during **scope definition,** determine the project's *talent needs* using **required skills analysis.**

Analyze Existing Resources

Identify all committed initial staffing, and document the initial project team roster during **organizational planning.** Determine *available resources,* using information from **project initiation** documentation such as a **project charter.** Describe the equipment, funding, and other resources that your project can depend on.

Assess the realistically available effort provided by committed project staff. Ask people about other commitments, anticipated time off, and any other factors that could reduce the amount of effort available. For extended team members, be realistic about how much effort "part time" on the project actually represents, and be skeptical of optimistic-sounding promises from staff members working on **multiple independent projects.** Develop an available resource profile similar to your required resource profile (again using a time-scaled histogram or a spreadsheet), and identify any differences between what you need and what you have. If your preliminary project schedule reveals significant *overcommitments,* attempt to resolve them through **resource leveling.** Determine which portions of the project plan are understaffed, and document your analysis with planning data.

Compare the skills and experience of the project team with the project skills analysis. Also, use **responsibility analysis** to align staff members with each project activity derived from the work breakdown structure. Identify *unmet resource requirements* that project work depends on, such as:

➤ Unavailable skills or inadequate experience levels

➤ Key project roles that are unstaffed

➤ Insufficient staffing levels

➤ Requirements for new or upgraded equipment

➤ Needed changes to the work environment

➤ Improvements to the communications infrastructure

➤ Inadequate funding for travel, support, or other needs

Overall, compare the total cost budget for your plan with the project resource goals from the project objective. If your plan is over budget, make adjustments, if possible, through **constraint management and plan optimization.** Identify any remaining difference.

Document Resource Plans

Capture specific *resource plans* based on committed resources, as part of overall **project plan development.** Formally document all ownership and responsibility commitments.

Specify how you plan to *meet unresolved resource requirements.* Options include:

➤ **Negotiating project changes** to timing or scope to align with available resources

➤ Additional **staff acquisition**

➤ Contracting for outside help through **procurement planning**

Add all resource issues that are not resolved to the *project risk list* during **risk identification.**

74 **Responsibility Analysis**

WHAT: Determining that all defined project activities have an owner, and if needed, sufficient additional staff.

WHEN: Project planning.

RESULTS: A two-dimensional matrix summarizing coverage and responsibilities for project work.

Roles

Define roles needed for the project activities, including:

➤ Owner (responsible for planning, reporting, and managing the work)

➤ Contributor (this category is often subdivided by function, such as marketing, support, construction, quality, finance)

➤ Approver (for sign-off)

➤ Input provider

➤ Reviewer, auditor

Matrix

Analyze the staffing for project activities using a two-dimensional matrix listing the defined project activities on one axis and the project staff by name on the other. Include an extra slot on the staffing axis to keep track of staffing needs that are not yet met. A simple example:

	Hawkeye	Margaret	Trapper	Radar	tbh
Activity 1.1.1	O		C	A	C
Activity 1.1.2	R	O			
Activity 1.2.1	C	C	O	R	CCC
Activity 1.2.2	A	O	C	C	

Analysis

Inspect the matrix to ensure that each activity has one, and only one, owner. For each activity, assess whether the staffing seems adequate and whether you believe that the contributors involved are capable of the work. For each individual, check to see he or she is not assigned more project responsibility, particularly activity ownership, than seems appropriate. Check that the talents available are consistent with your **required skills analysis.** Use the "to be hired" (tbh) data to assist in **staff acquisition.**

75 **Return on Investment Analysis**

WHAT: Analyzing project costs and benefits.

WHEN: Project initiation and planning.

RESULTS: A quantitative assessment of a project's overall financial value.

ROI Basis and Types of Analysis

All project return on investment (ROI) estimates are **project predictive metrics.** ROI analysis depends on contrasting *costs and benefits* (project-related monetary outflows and inflows). Because they are based on future benefits estimates, which are often unreliable, the accuracy of ROI metrics can be highly variable.

Most ROI methods are based on the *time value of money,* assuming a discount rate (or interest rate) that makes a sum of money in the future less valuable than the same sum of money today. The formula for this is: $PV = FV/(1 + i)^n$, where: PV is the present value, FV is the future value, i is the periodic interest rate, and n is the number of periods. (If the period is a year and the interest rate is 5 percent [.05] per year, then $1.00 today is equal to $1.05 in one year.)

There are a number of ways to calculate ROI, and each has benefits and drawbacks. Although all ROI measures rely on similar data, they may yield different results when used to compare projects. Typical *methods* include simple payback, discounted payback, net present value, and internal rate of return.

SIMPLE PAYBACK

The easiest method for project ROI assessment calculates a *payback period* assuming no time value of money. Project costs are estimated using **cost budgeting.** Forecasts of project benefits, savings, or revenues following project completion are then made sufficiently far into the future, until the cumulative value of the benefits balances the project costs. The payback period is the time required for the project to pay for itself. Benefits: Simple payback is easy to calculate and can be validated against actual data in a reasonable time frame. Drawbacks: It ignores any benefits following payback, and it ignores project magnitude.

DISCOUNTED PAYBACK

This method is identical to simple payback, but uses a *discount rate*, so estimates in the future are not worth as much in the present. Because project costs are in the near future and project benefits are more distant, the discounted payback period is always longer than the simple payback period. For short projects, the difference is negligible, but for longer projects it can be substantial. Benefits and drawbacks are similar to those for simple payback.

NET PRESENT VALUE

Net present value (NPV) uses the same process as discounted payback analysis, but it continues past the break-even point. NPV is based on the project budget, but considers all the estimated benefits for the life of the project deliverable. Instead of estimating the amount of time required to recover costs, NPV estimates the result of adding up all the discounted benefits minus all the discounted costs, delivering an estimate of total project *monetary worth*. Benefits: NPV can be used to compare projects with very different financial profiles and time scales. Drawbacks: NPV favors large projects over smaller ones, requires more estimates, and the time frame for validation is very long.

INTERNAL RATE OF RETURN

Internal rate of return (IRR) is the most complex of the ROI metrics. IRR uses the same estimates for costs and returns required to calculate total NPV, but instead of assuming an interest rate and calculating an overall project value, IRR assumes a present value of zero and determines the *implied interest rate*. Benefits: IRR is useful for comparing projects of different sizes and lengths. Drawbacks: IRR analysis requires financial software; more data are needed; and, like NPV, it takes a long time to validate.

76 Rewards and Recognition

WHAT: Formal acknowledgment of individual and team accomplishments.

WHEN: Throughout a project, but particularly at project closure.

RESULTS: Better cooperation and teamwork, and successful current and future projects.

Generally, rewards and recognition are most effective when *tailored to the individual* or team, so determine in advance whether recognition should be public or non-public and verify what rewards are likely to be most appreciated through **communicating informally.**

Intangible Rewards and Recognition

Recognition expressed in ways involving little or no out-of-pocket cost is a powerful way to increase **motivation.** Intangible rewards should be frequent, and are most effective when they are unexpected, so employ them randomly. Typical examples include:

➤ *Thank people personally* for their accomplishments. Do it face-to-face if possible, or by telephone or e-mail for **global teams.** Keep alert and express appreciation even for small things.

➤ *Use team members' names* in **performance reporting, lessons learned,** and other project documents when discussing results. Be specific, and include a summary of why the accomplishments matter.

➤ *Formally recognize achievements and results* on **matrix teams** to the team member's management, in writing. Submit thorough reports on team members in advance of their performance evaluations.

➤ *Thank people in public meetings* (if culturally appropriate) for significant contributions.

➤ *Discuss individual and team results* in project status meetings, **project reviews,** and **presentations.**

➤ *Let people represent the project team* at management or customer meetings.

➤ *Expand responsibility* within the team.

➤ *Issue certificates or tokens* (buttons, pens, and other small items) to acknowledge performance.

Tangible Rewards and Recognition (Public)

Public recognition using rewards with financial cost can be effective if the rewards are appreciated and aligned with individual preferences. Expensive events and items that people do not like can actually be demotivating, as can undesired public attention. Some examples of effective rewards are:

➤ *Team-planned events or celebrations* to commemorate project successes

➤ *Nomination of individuals or teams* for monetary or other award programs, either internal or external to the organization

➤ *Substantial rewards for performance* such as clothing, food, or other visible gifts

➤ *Travel and support for attendance* at professional conferences or training classes

➤ *Promotion* or other formal expansion of responsibility

Tangible Rewards and Recognition (Non-public)

Most rewards involving money are private. Monetary rewards are most effective when infrequent, because when they are expected they are no longer perceived as rewards. Based on the project structure and the authority of the project leader, some of these are:

➤ *Recommendations for salary increases*

➤ *Financial rewards* such as bonuses or stock options

➤ *Gift certificates,* allowances for meals, tickets to an event, or other individual rewards that cost money

Where programs for such recognition exist, take full advantage of them.

77 **Risk Identification** (PMBOK® 11.2)

WHAT: Documenting and diagnosing potential project problems.

WHEN: Project planning and control.

RESULTS: A robust list of known potential project problems.

Risk History

Review *previous project problems,* historical data, **lessons learned,** and databases containing risk information, both inside your organization and from public sources. Find and note the things that went wrong.

Project Planning

Throughout **project plan development,** uncover project risks as you *analyze the work.* Follow the overall processes defined in **risk management planning.**
   In **scope planning** and **scope definition,** consider *scope risks,* such as:

➤ Technical system complexity

➤ Conflicting or inconsistent specifications

➤ Extreme performance, reliability, or quality requirements

➤ Mandatory use of new technology

➤ Requirements to invent or discover new capabilities

➤ Incomplete or poorly defined acceptance criteria

➤ Unclear or potentially changing customer requirements

➤ Impact of component availability or defects

➤ External sourcing for a key subcomponent or tool

➤ Overall size of the project work breakdown structure

➤ Large work segments that resist breakdown

In **activity definition, activity duration estimating, activity sequencing,** and **schedule development,** identify *schedule risks,* looking for:

➤ Activities without a willing owner

➤ Activities with durations longer than two weeks

➤ Activities with uncertain duration estimates

➤ Activities with significant worst-case (pessimistic PERT) estimates

- Activities on the project critical path or with minimal float
- Simultaneous critical activities
- Activities or milestones with multiple predecessors
- Activities with external dependencies and interfaces
- Scheduled work beyond the realistic planning horizon
- Crossfunctional and subcontracted activities

During **organizational planning, resource planning, staff acquisition, cost estimating, procurement planning,** and **solicitation planning,** document *resource risks,* including:

- Activities with unknown staffing
- Activities requiring skills not currently available
- Activities dependent on a specific key individual
- Activities staffed using part-time or remote team members
- Activities with uncertain cost estimates
- Understaffed activities or groups of activities
- Outsourcing and contract risks

Risk Discovery Processes

Uncover additional risks outside the overall planning process by determining other risks, such as:

- Communications or language difficulties
- Regulatory or other external changes
- Market or user requirement shifts
- Business reorganization or loss of project sponsorship
- Loss of proprietary or confidential information

Augment the risk list of identified risks with the whole project team. Gather to **brainstorm** additional risks by:

- Examining project assumptions and constraints
- Discussing all worst-case activity duration and cost estimates
- Analyzing risk scenarios
- Assessing the impact of potential delays and slips

Document Risks

Create a *risk register* containing all identified risks. Clearly describe each listed risk. Define the potential consequences to the project for each risk. For every listed risk, identify a trigger event that reveals that the risk has occurred or is about to occur.

78 **Risk Management Planning** (PMBOK® 11.1)

WHAT: Documenting how you will deal with project risks.

WHEN: Project planning.

RESULTS: Understanding of project stakeholder risk tolerance and a systematic approach for dealing with project risk.

Stakeholder Risk Tolerance

Different organizations have radically different *perceptions of risk.* Assess the willingness to accept risk among the sponsors, and team members through:

➤ Meetings

➤ Discussions and interviews

➤ Examination of organizational policies

➤ Review of the project charter and other initial project documents

Test project assumptions in discussions with project stakeholders by asking questions for clarification. *Validate risk tolerances* with project stakeholders.

Determine Risk Management Process

Ensure that risk management is embedded in the processes used for **project plan development** and **project plan execution.** Use templates and standards for risk identification and management, and *integrate risk activities* in the project methodologies and development methods you will use. Use historical project information and **lessons learned** on earlier work as a foundation for risk management.

Risk management on large programs represents a significant effort. As part of **cost budgeting,** secure *commitment for funding* and staffing of risk management.

Adopt an overall process including:

➤ **Risk identification**

➤ **Qualitative risk analysis** and **quantitative risk analysis**

➤ **Risk response planning**

➤ **Risk monitoring and control**

For small projects, risk planning may be informal, but for large, complex projects, you may want to document your *risk management plan*. Typical risk management plans include:

- ➤ A summary of your risk management approach
- ➤ Stakeholder information
- ➤ Planning processes, tools, and **project metrics**
- ➤ Risk management standards, definitions, and report formats
- ➤ The risk-related activities during periodic **project reviews**
- ➤ Planned project risk-related activities

Risk Surveys and Overall Assessment

Use *risk questionnaires,* surveys, or other methods to assess overall project risk. Probe for exposures related to the project objectives, customers and users, development methods, and **project infrastructure.**

Using hardcopy forms, online surveys, or interviews, identify sources of overall exposure for the project, and *propose changes* to reduce systemic project risks.

79 **Risk Monitoring and Control** (PMBOK® 11.6)

WHAT: Tracking identified project risk triggers and responding as necessary.

WHEN: Project execution and control.

RESULTS: Fewer project surprises, and prompt and effective response to problems.

Monitor Risks

This process is part of **project plan execution.** Based on your **risk management planning,** both the known risks documented during **risk identification** and unanticipated risks that arise must be monitored and resolved. The owners of each contingency plan developed as part of **risk response planning** monitor for specific *risk triggers,* and overall project **status collection** and **plan variance analysis** provide general risk monitoring.

Use *trend analysis* of project **performance reporting** and **project metrics** such as **earned value management** to identify potential future risks.

Periodically reevaluate project risks during **project reviews.** Update the risk register, analyze and prioritize the risks, and plan responses for all significant *new risks.*

Risk Response

When a risk occurs, whether anticipated or not, *respond promptly.* If there is a contingency plan established for the problem, begin its execution as soon as practical.

For risks that were passively accepted or are unexpected, involve the project *team members* in the response planning.

Develop a response to the risk using techniques for **schedule control** and **cost control,** and attempt to *recover quickly.* Seek workarounds and ad hoc responses that are consistent with your **project infrastructure** decisions.

If *major changes* are necessary, validate the response using **integrated change control** processes before committing to it. Discuss any major changes with the project sponsor and appropriate stakeholders. If necessary, use **problem escalation** to obtain approval. Very major risk responses may result in new **project baseline setting.**

Inform the project team and appropriate stakeholders of your plans and *implement the risk response.*

Verify Fix

Following your response, monitor to ensure that your response obtained the *expected results* and did not lead to adverse unforeseen consequences.

If the risk situation continues, seek a better solution through *additional planning* for risk response.

Document Risk History

As part of risk control, *update project documents* that are affected by your responses and communicate the results of your efforts in project **performance reporting.**

Add the information on encountered risks to your project information archive, and add descriptions of new risk situations encountered to *risk checklists,* templates, and databases. Analyze risk data during **project reviews** and in capturing **lessons learned.**

80 **Risk Response Planning** (PMBOK® 11.5)

WHAT: Determining how best to deal with high-severity known risks.

WHEN: Project planning, execution, and control.

RESULTS: Adjustments to the project plan dealing with preventable risks, and contingency plans for other risks.

Risk Triggers and Timeline

Read down the risk register sorted using **qualitative risk analysis** or **quantitative risk analysis.** *Select* the significant risks that you will manage (typically, these will have at least moderate probability and impact).

Review the *trigger events* for these risks, and determine the point or points on the project timeline when the risk is most likely to occur. Risk management involves prevention and planning in advance of the trigger and risk responses after the trigger.

Risk Categorization

Seek the *root cause* of each risk to be managed. Use **cause-and-effect analysis** to determine the source(s) of the risks, striving to understand the risks better and to determine whether they are controllable or uncontrollable.

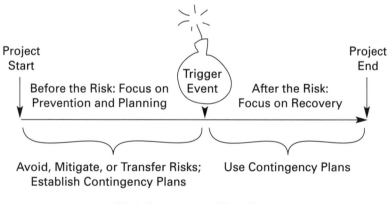

Risk Response Timeline

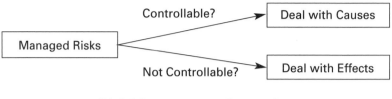

Risk Management Strategies

When risk sources are under your control, *prevention strategies* may provide solutions. Probe deeply to uncover the source of the risk, not just the symptoms.

For uncontrollable risks, risk management requires *response strategies*.

Dealing with Causes

Risk prevention strategies include avoidance, mitigation, and transfer.

Risk *avoidance* involves replanning the project to remove the source of the risk entirely. Avoiding risks may involve:

➤ Scope risks: Committing to the minimum acceptable deliverable, eliminating new technology, buying instead of making components

➤ Schedule risks: Reducing the number of activity dependencies, scheduling the high-risk activities early, decomposing lengthy activities

➤ Resource risks: Getting names and commitments for all work, building needed skills, eliminating overcommitments

For risks that you cannot plan around, **brainstorm** ideas for *mitigation,* reducing the risk probability or impact (or both). Mitigation tactics include:

➤ General: Improving communication, securing strong **sponsorship,** keeping users involved, documenting and enforcing **project priorities**

➤ Scope: Freezing specifications, rigorously managing **scope change control,** building models and prototypes, keeping all documents current

➤ Schedule: Using "expected" **activity duration estimating,** scheduling the highest-priority work early, holding **project reviews,** tracking rigorously

➤ Resources: Avoiding overtime, building trust and teamwork, rigorously managing outsourced work

For some financial risks, *transfer* may be effective. For some projects, insurance against large unexpected expense may be justified in the project budget.

Examine all ideas for risk prevention, comparing their *costs* (such as time, money, and effort) with their *benefits* of risk reduction. Select the ideas that lower project risk impact at justifiable cost, and update your project plan.

Recovery

When risk prevention is impossible or not cost effective, plan for *response*. Responses are either determined in advance (contingency planning) or coincident with the risk event (passive acceptance).

For most significant risks you cannot prevent, prepare *contingency plans*. Use your **project plan development** process to create a plan for recovering from each risk. Ideas include:

➤ General: Using schedule or resource reserve, **negotiating project changes**

➤ Schedule: Postponing noncritical activities, shifting staff, rescheduling work

➤ Resources: Using overtime, outsourcing, getting staff from lower priority projects

➤ Scope: Relaxing some specifications, reprioritizing features

For each contingency plan, identify *triggers and owners*. Assign an owner to monitor each risk, and clearly specify the trigger event that the owner will monitor.

For some risks, it may be impractical to plan specifically for risk recovery. When a specific risk response is not an option, you may choose to *passively accept* the risk, proceeding with no specific risk response. This tactic is generally used for very minor risks (including all the risks on your risk register that you chose not to manage).

Overall

Document all risks and keep them *visible*. Post a "top ten" list.

Use contingency planning and other risk data to establish schedule and budget *reserves*.

81 **Schedule Control** (PMBOK® 6.5)

WHAT: Monitoring project activities and managing project timing.

WHEN: Project execution and control.

RESULTS: Accurate project activity tracking and plan adjustments as required to meet milestones and deadlines.

Determine Status and Analyze Variances

Schedule control is central to **project plan execution.** It follows **status collection** and **plan variance analysis** in the project tracking cycle. It is necessary in any cycle where you discover a significant schedule variance. For each variance, review its *root cause and impact* on the project timeline. Determine whether the impact is a one-time or short-term issue, or whether the root cause is a longer term chronic problem.

Plan Responses

Review your **project infrastructure** decisions and **integrated change control** process to *ensure consistency* with agreed-on principles.

Involve the project *team members* in the response planning; engage as many perspectives and points of view as practical.

Depending on the severity of the problem and the nature of its root cause, the *type of response* may be:

➤ A minor change that preserves the **project objective**

➤ Implementation of a contingency plan developed during **risk response planning**

➤ A major change to the project

For *short-term* schedule problems, consider "brute force" solutions, such as working overtime in the evenings or on non-workdays.

For more significant problems, **brainstorm** approaches that could bring the project back on schedule. Explore options using the processes of **project plan development,** especially **constraint management and plan optimization.** Develop plans that deal with the root cause of the problem, not just the symptoms. **Software tools for project management** may be very useful in exploring "what if?" planning scenarios. Avoid adopting the first alternative you develop; work to generate a *number of credible responses.* Typical responses include:

- ➤ Changing the logical flow of the work
- ➤ Breaking future activities into smaller, simultaneous tasks
- ➤ Finding new, faster ways to do project work
- ➤ Borrowing team members from less critical work
- ➤ Working extra hours
- ➤ Getting available team members (or the project leader) to assist in slipping activities
- ➤ Reducing the scope of the project deliverable
- ➤ Responses that were effective in similar past situations

For problems that cannot be solved using conventional analysis, use **creative problem solving.** Allocate a reasonable amount of time to plan a response, but avoid "analysis paralysis." Set a time limit for planning and use systematic **decision making** to choose the *best idea* available within that limit.

Take Action and Document Results

Validate the response you select before you implement it. Verify that your proposal is consistent with your **project priorities.** If the response involves changes to the deliverable, get approval for it through **scope change control.** Discuss any major changes with the project sponsor and appropriate stakeholders. If necessary, use **problem escalation** to obtain approval. Very major changes may require new **project baseline setting.**

Inform the project team and appropriate stakeholders of your plans and *implement the response.*

Following implementation, monitor to ensure that your response obtained the *expected results* and did not lead to adverse unforeseen consequences. If problems persist, seek a better solution through additional planning.

Update any project and *planning documents* that are affected by the actions, and communicate the results of your efforts in project **performance reporting.**

82 **Schedule Development** (PMBOK® 6.4)

WHAT: Developing a project schedule based on calendar dates.

WHEN: Project planning, execution, and control.

RESULTS: Identification of critical paths, and a schedule that can be used for analysis, negotiation, and tracking.

Document Relevant Non-Project Dates and Factors

Schedule development is a central component of **project plan development.** It combines **activity duration estimates** with **activity dependencies** to determine *calendar dates* for the project, based on bottom-up analysis.

Begin the process by creating a *project calendar.* Identify all significant dates important to the project, including the project start date, any project constraints, interim and final deadlines, and any key dates when your project interacts with other scheduled work. Also include information about the project team, such as:

➤ *Weekends* you plan to work (if any)

➤ *Holidays* and other non-workdays—for all locations doing project work

➤ Each team member's *planned vacations* and other timing conflicts

➤ *Organizational meetings,* key dates, and events

➤ Planned *site closures*

➤ Scheduled *equipment downtime* for maintenance

If you are using a **software tool for project management,** *enter calendar information* into the tool's database. Establish the calendar before you enter project activity estimates and dependency data.

Analyze and Document the Project Schedule

By adding duration estimate information to a project activity network diagram showing dependencies, you can determine the project's *critical path* (or paths). A critical path has the longest total duration of any continuous connected string of activities in the project. Critical path analysis may be done either manually or using computer software. Manual analysis is impractical for projects larger than about 100 activities.

Critical path methodology (CPM) relies on *two separate analyses* of the project: a forward analysis pass to calculate the earliest date each activity could be scheduled and a reverse analysis pass to calculate the latest date for each activity consistent with the end date of the forward pass.

The *early schedule* for each activity is determined first, working forward in time along each of the project network's activity paths. It defines the dates when work can begin and should end. The early schedule is normally used for project execution.

Following the determination of the early schedule, the same kind of analysis is done, working backward in time from the end of the longest (or critical) activity path to determine the *late schedule* for each activity. The late start and late finish dates show the most delayed timing for each activity that does not extend the project critical path.

Project activities that have late schedules showing dates after their early schedules are identified as *noncritical*, and the timing difference between the two calculated schedules is called float or slack.

Project activities with zero float have identical early and late schedule dates, and are therefore *critical*. All activities with no float are connected to other critical activities through dependencies, and the linkages define one or more project critical paths. (Activities are also critical when they have negative float, which occurs when the project deadline is an earlier date than the end date for the calculated critical path.)

Computer scheduling tools *automate the analysis* (which can be quite tedious) and generally display the noncritical activities in soothing blue and the critical activities in scary red.

Computers are able to generate time-scaled bar charts of project activities, also called *Gantt charts* (after their originator, Henry Gantt). Simple Gantt charts can display dependencies (as in the example), but network charts are best for showing workflow for large projects.

ID	Task Name	Duration	Predecessors	Month 1				Month 2					Month 3	
				W1	W2	W3	W4	W5	W6	W7	W8	W9	W10	W11
1	Project Skywalker	50 days												
2	Start	0 days												
3	Determine Specifications	5 days	2											
4	Design System	5 days	3											
5	Develop Test Plan	2 days	3											
6	Document System	7 days	4											
7	Buy Hardware	10 days	4											
8	Write Software	15 days	4,5											
9	Identify Test Users	3 days	5											
10	Build System	10 days	6,7,8,9											
11	System Built	0 days	10											
12	Install User Systems	5 days	11											
13	Perform Tests	2 days	12											
14	Fix User Test Defects	7 days	13											
15	Release System	1 day	14											
16	End	0 days	15											

Adjust Plans to Meet Project Constraints

With activities are aligned with the calendar, work in parallel becomes visible. *Modify activity timing* to resolve timing problems. Adjust dependencies and delay work as necessary to avoid simultaneous conflicting activities. Change activity timing as necessary to manage dependencies and interfaces among **multiple dependent projects.** Analyze the effort requirements needed throughout the project timeline, and use **resource leveling** to extend the schedule if necessary when the work requires more effort than the project team can deliver.

Refine the plan to *manage risks,* through **risk identification,** analysis, and **risk response planning.** Add any new activities for risk avoidance and risk mitigation to the project plan, and adjust the schedule accordingly.

The schedule resulting from timing, resource, and risk analysis rarely supports the deadline in the **project objective.** Work to *minimize schedule issues* through **constraint management and plan optimization.** If an acceptable alternative plan emerges from your analysis, document it, and use it for **project baseline setting.**

If your best planning efforts fail to support stated project objectives and constraints, develop several realistic project *plan alternatives* that are close, and use them to **negotiate project changes.**

Document and Use the Schedule

Alternatives to the Gantt chart for *schedule documentation* include tables, computer spreadsheets, databases, notebooks, and project dictionaries.

Computer simulations of project risk, such as automated tools for Program Evaluation and Review Technique (PERT), display project schedules using distributions and histograms, showing the probabilities associated with project completion on given calendar dates.

Use the early activity schedule dates for **project plan execution,** and keep the schedule current through **schedule control.**

Revalidate the overall schedule periodically during **project reviews,** especially on lengthy projects.

83 **Scope Change Control** (PMBOK® 5.5)

WHAT: Managing specification changes to the project deliverables.

WHEN: Project execution and control.

RESULTS: Acceptance of changes that represent net benefits, and rejection or deferral of other proposed changes.

Change Process

Once the project **scope planning** and the **project baseline setting** have been validated, use a *documented process* for scope change control. Managing the specifications of project deliverables is a central component of **integrated change control.** Although the formality of the control process may vary, even on short projects a written process will assist in maintaining scope stability. Effective processes default to a response of "reject," forcing all proposed changes to establish their business value before becoming part of the project.

Effective change control also requires appropriate *authority* for the people who will review, analyze, and decide on proposed changes. To guard against frequent unnecessary change, approvers need the power to say "no" (or at least "not yet") and make it stick.

Change Proposal

Scope changes usually are needed to solve project problems or to respond to opportunities. Whatever the source, document any proposed changes *in writing*, and include information such as:

➤ The situation that makes a change necessary

➤ A quantitative assessment of benefits from the change

➤ The estimated impact of the change on schedule, cost, and other factors

➤ Specific resources needed for the change

Following submission, review each submitted change proposal for *completeness*. If the information is unclear or data are missing, return the request to the author for revision before considering it further.

When the proposal is satisfactory, *log* the submission and set a time for its review. Provide information on the change to the people who are responsible for evaluation, review, and approval, and let the submitter know when to expect a decision. Some find it useful to categorize changes as small (negligible

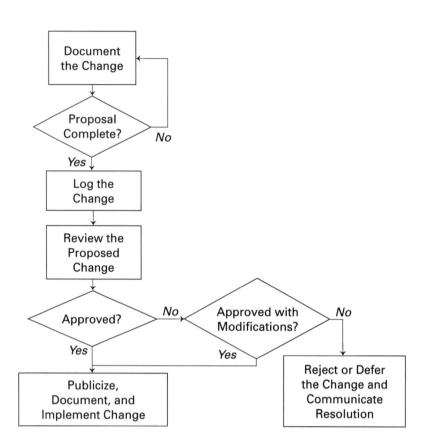

effect on the deliverable or project), medium (some change to scope but low impact to the project plans), or large (significant change to both scope and the project baseline).

Review Change(s)

For each change, review the original situation and verify that the change proposed is the best response available. *Validate* that the change proposed is feasible, and that it is likely to obtain the desired result and avoid unintended consequences.

Analyze the *impact* of the proposed change. Determine the effect on:

➤ The project schedule

➤ Additional project activities and effort

➤ Costs for additional equipment, components, training, rework, and scrap

- ➤ Contracts for purchasing of materials or outsourced services
- ➤ Customer satisfaction
- ➤ **Project priorities**
- ➤ Other projects

Assess the *benefits* of the proposed change. For problem-solving changes, determine avoided expense or schedule slippage. If the change relates to an external factor (modified legal requirements, new standards, competitor actions), estimate the impact of failing to respond. Project changes that respond to opportunities must be supported by credible (not optimistic) estimates for increased sales, value, or usefulness as a result of the change. If a change is in response to a customer request, determine why it is needed and what it is worth to them.

Analyze the *net benefits* of each change. Determine the overall value of the change by contrasting the costs and other consequences of accepting the change with its reasonably expected benefits.

Use a consistent process for **decision-making,** and *make decisions* promptly. For each potential change, there are four alternatives: approval, approval with modification, deferral, and rejection. Reject all changes that lack a compelling, credible business case. Before approving a beneficial change, verify that all of it is necessary, and determine if it might be deferred to a later time. Approve changes sparingly, and only when supported by significant business needs.

Communicate and Document

Document each change request decision in writing. Note the reason for the decision and *communicate the results* to team members, appropriate stakeholders, and to the submitters.

Log the disposition of each change, and add the change decisions to your project information archive, for use in **project reviews** and analysis of **lessons learned.**

Update project plans and documentation as necessary, and revalidate the project baseline following any accepted major changes.

Implement all approved changes promptly, and monitor for expected results and any unintended consequences.

84 Scope Definition (WBS) (PMBOK® 5.3)

WHAT: Creating a hierarchical, comprehensive description of the project work.

WHEN: Project planning, execution, and control.

RESULTS: A project work breakdown structure (WBS) that serves as the foundation for realistic planning and meaningful tracking.

Prepare

Defining scope is a *team process*. Identifying project work completely requires the perspective of all contributors—from other functions, from support organizations, and from people who may only be involved later in the project. Involve the core project team and other stakeholders who can help in understanding the project.

Plan the *logistics*. For large projects, scope definition may take several days. Allocate at least two hours for even modest projects, and seek a quiet place away from your normal work area with ample room and open wall space. Provide necessary supplies, such as thick, dark pens, yellow sticky notes, and tape or pins to post large sheets of paper on the walls.

Assemble *project documentation* from **project initiation** and **scope planning,** such as the **project objective, project priorities, project charter,** and **project vision.** Review the **user needs assessment,** and define the project acceptance criteria. Also provide work breakdowns developed for earlier similar projects, and any relevant WBS templates.

Before beginning to decompose the work with your team, break *larger programs* into smaller projects that can be assigned to teams of at most twelve people.

Identify Project Work

The goal of the scope definition process is to describe the project in much smaller pieces, or *work packages*. A project WBS is a structured hierarchy, with work packages at lower levels representing less and less of the overall project. The lowest-level work packages are often called "tasks" or "activities," but terminology varies widely.

A WBS is typically developed by breaking the overall project deliverable into major subsets of work, and then continuing the process of *decomposition* down through multiple levels. Identify work through **brainstorming** and using lists of activities from earlier projects.

Document each work package on a separate sticky note, giving each one a *verb–noun description.* The verb defines the effort, and the noun identifies the deliverable. Examples are "Test user interfaces" and "Interview customers."

Strive for as *complete* a set of activities as possible. Include key project management tasks and any training, integration, and testing activities. Identify missing tasks that must come before or after tasks already identified. Break large tasks into shorter tasks.

Continue the breakdown process until lowest-level activities are:

➤ *Small.* Guidelines vary, but strive for durations of between two and twenty workdays or effort of no more than 80 person-hours. Project work broken down to this level of detail provides a good foundation for **activity duration estimating, cost estimating, schedule development, risk identification,** and **performance reporting.**

➤ *Assignable.* Each activity can be unambiguously assigned to a single owner.

➤ *Measurable.* Completion criteria are specific and clear.

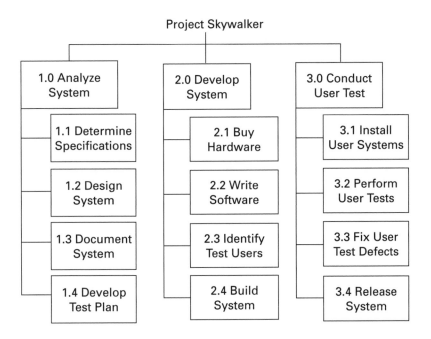

Organize the Work

Once activities are identified and documented, use the sticky notes to develop a hierarchy that shows the overall project in a logical structure. Major deliverables are commonly used for the first level below the project objective, but there are other possible organizing principles for project work:

➤ By organizational function (marketing, R&D, manufacturing)

➤ By discipline (carpentry, masonry, plumbing, electrical, painting)

➤ By skill set (programming, accounting, marketing)

➤ By geography (Stuttgart, Bangalore, Topeka, Taipei, Bogota)

➤ By life-cycle phase (analyze, design, build, test, deploy)

When your WBS is organized in a tree structure, test each lower level for *aggregation;* ensure that the decomposition is equivalent to the work package it branches from. Work breakdowns are most easily understood and used when work packages are broken down into seven or fewer parts. WBS branches often vary widely in levels and complexity.

Document and Use

Format the WBS in a *graphical display* or indented outline.

Use the WBS as a basis for **project plan development** and for **status collection** throughout the project. Update your WBS during **project reviews.**

85 Scope Planning (PMBOK® 5.2)

WHAT: Formally specifying the project deliverables.

WHEN: Project initiation and planning.

RESULTS: A clearly written scope statement and specifications for all deliverables.

Assemble Deliverable Data

Collect project information that emerges from the **project initiation** process. Input data for scope planning include:

➤ **Project objective** statement

➤ **Project charter**

➤ Constraints and assumptions

➤ High-level deliverable definitions

Involve the core team and others as needed to review the available information.

Assess project data for completeness, considering aspects such as:

➤ **User needs assessment**

➤ Regulatory, legal, and standards compliance

➤ Analysis of alternatives and competition

➤ Measurable performance and other goals

➤ Delivery, support, installation, distribution, and other logistical issues

➤ Technical and other risks

Document what is known about each project deliverable, and *identify data gaps.*

Resolve Unknowns

For missing user needs information, conduct or encourage **customer interviews** or **market research.** For other significant *missing information,* add activities to the project work breakdown structure during scope definition. If needed information remains unavailable, note it in project **risk identification.**

For each project deliverable, minimize fuzzy specifications using an "*Is/Is not*" list. Document all requirements and constraints that must be met in the

"Is" part of the list. List features and aspects of the scope that are desirable, but not required, in the "Is not" part of the list. Include all project wants initially in the "Is not" list.

Define *measurable standards* for each project deliverable and define the process for testing during **scope verification.** Identify who must approve the results of testing and sign off for approval.

Document Scope

Write a high-level *scope statement* that includes a brief description of all project deliverables.

For *each deliverable,* specify:

➤ What it is, and what it is not

➤ Needed functionality

➤ Interface and usability requirements

➤ Quantitative standards for performance and reliability

➤ Documentation, training, and support needs

➤ Acceptance tests

Document the *scope management* process (or adopt an existing one) that will be used for **scope change control** throughout the project.

Obtain Approval

Validate the scope statement, deliverable definitions, and your scope management plan with the project sponsor, and with users, customers, and other stakeholders as needed. Resolve misunderstandings early in planning to avoid later rework and changes. When appropriate, get formal sign-off on the scope requirements.

Use the scope planning data for **scope definition,** other **project plan development** activities, and **integrated change control.**

86 Scope Verification (PMBOK® 5.4)

WHAT: Obtaining formal acceptance of project deliverables.

WHEN: Project execution, control, and closure.

RESULTS: Sign-off by customers and others as necessary for intermediate and final project outputs.

Review Acceptance Criteria

As part of **schedule development,** *incorporate activities* for testing, validation, and formally obtaining agreement that project deliverables meet their requirements. This is an important part of **administrative closure,** but verification activities may occur throughout a project. Coordinate scope verification with **quality assurance** and **quality control** efforts.

In addition to the timing, review the *specifications* and performance measures that were outlined during **scope planning.** Document the processes, standards, and equipment required for acceptance testing, and ensure that the resources will be available and operating properly when they are needed. If requirements are modified through **scope change control,** update the specifications and acceptance tests as necessary.

Test and Evaluate

As project outputs are completed, do an *internal assessment* within the project team, inspecting, examining, and checking the results. Identify any defects or problems and revise your plans to correct the deficiencies.

When project deliverables require *external validation,* conduct tests to verify that the deliverables meet all the requirements set by the people who must sign off on them.

If the project deliverables are consistent with the specifications, get *formal approval.* If the deliverables fail to meet the measurement standards, do one of the following:

➤ Address the issues promptly and obtain sign-off

➤ **Negotiate project changes** consistent with results and obtain sign-off

➤ Capture status information and plan for additional effort

Document Sign-off (or Status)

Incorporate the *outcome* of your scope verification effort in project **performance reporting,** and add the results of all inspections and tests to your project management information system.

87 Software Tools for Project Management

WHAT: Using computer applications to facilitate project management processes and communications.

WHEN: Throughout a project.

RESULTS: Lower overhead and effort, and better quality project information.

Planning and Scheduling

Determine your needs. Small projects can be managed easily without specialized software, and the overhead of learning and using a new application can represent a net increase in overall work. Projects longer than a few months or with more than 100 tasks in their **activity definition** easily justify the use of at least a low-end project management tool. Considerations in selecting software include:

➤ *Cost* (software, training, support, upgrades, or other expenses)

➤ *Adoption by peers* (with resulting access to local expertise)

➤ *Ease of use* (installation, learning curve, operation, updates)

➤ *Compatibility* with organizational standards and related applications

➤ Need for specialized *risk analysis*

➤ Extensive *resource analysis* and tracking requirements

➤ *Customized reporting* capability

➤ Requirements for *import and export* of project information

➤ *Multi-project (program) analysis*

➤ *WWW or remote network access*

Adopt a tool that *meets your needs,* without a lot of excess capability that increases the cost and makes operation confusing. For projects lasting six months to one year and having a modest number of external dependencies, midrange tools (such as Scitor Project Scheduler, Microsoft Project, and CA SuperProject) are generally adequate. For larger projects or projects needing more access and analysis capabilities, high-end tools are a better choice (examples include products from Primavera, Niku Project Workbench, and Welcom Open Plan Professional). Although these packages are more costly and difficult to master, they offer capabilities not present in the midrange scheduling tools.

Learn the tool. To use any project management tool fully, you need to find a mentor or attend training. Build your skills through practice and use of the tool.

Increase efficiency through sharing experiences with others who use the same software. Create templates that contain all the standard activities typically included in project work in the format of your tool. Share the templates with others and improve them over time.

Use the tool effectively. A project scheduling tool is merely a database with some specialized reporting and analysis capabilities. While it cannot plan or manage your project for you, it can make your job easier. The tool's database can help in collecting and organizing project information for **project plan development.** If you build your plans using bottom-up analysis of project work (as opposed to "must start on," top-down imposed deadlines), the scheduling tool will be a great help in "what if?" analysis, **constraint management and plan optimization,** and **risk response planning.**

Track the project. Use the tool to collect and compare actual schedule and cost information with plans for performance reporting. Use the software throughout **project plan execution** to support **schedule control** and **cost control.**

Communication Tools

All communication technology works best when supported periodically with *face-to-face interaction.* Build **teamwork** and trust to enhance your use of technology.

Consider all available *communications capabilities* in your **communications planning.** Use technology to support **information distribution** and archiving of project data needed by the project team.

When working with *distributed teams,* adopt and use **virtual team technical tools** to effectively maintain teamwork and accelerate project progress.

Other Tools

Risk management software packages (such as Risk+ and @Risk) are useful for **quantitative risk analysis.**

Decision support software (examples are Crystal Ball and Expert Choice) can be very effective for **decision making** in complex project situations.

Issue tracking systems, either purchased or based on a spreadsheet or other database, may be needed for effective **integrated change management** on large programs.

Time and resource tracking software can support detailed reporting requirements for government and some commercial projects. They can also support collection of **earned value management** metrics.

88 Solicitation (PMBOK® 12.3)

WHAT: Identifying and contacting potential suppliers and collecting their bids and proposals.

WHEN: Project initiation and planning.

RESULTS: Supplier submissions that meet your project requirements.

Identify Potential Suppliers

Based on **solicitation planning,** determine how to identify suppliers who will be interested in your work and capable of following through. Review lists of known suppliers, looking especially for those who have succeeded in the past. Use your personal network to discover what others are doing, both in your organization and in other places where you know peers through past work or professional association. To find a sufficient number of qualified respondents, it may be necessary to advertise, post information on the WWW, or involve specialists to locate suppliers. *List the potential responders,* including the individuals involved if they are known.

Distribute the RFP

Send the *request for proposal* (RFP), or similar document, to each potential bidder you identified as well as to those who respond to any public announcements. Ideally, you should send out a sufficient number to ensure three or more responses. Allow enough time between receipt of the RFP and the proposal due date to permit a comprehensive response. Request confirmation of RFP delivery.

Manage the Bidding Process

Encourage *communication.* Request early questions or clarification of anything in the RFP that is not clear. Reply promptly to all inquiries, and provide copies of the questions and your responses to all prospective bidders. If appropriate, schedule meetings or bidder conferences, providing "virtual" access via teleconference or computer networking when necessary.

Approximately one week before proposals are due, send a *reminder* to each potential supplier.

Receive the Proposals

As proposals arrive, check them quickly for completeness, and formally *acknowledge receipt* to the bidders. If time remains, inform bidders of any proposal defects. If proposals arrive late, determine how you will deal with them and communicate the status to the bidders.

89 Solicitation Planning (PMBOK® 12.2)

WHAT: Determining the requirements, decision criteria, and selection process to be used for outsourcing project work.

WHEN: Project initiation and planning.

RESULTS: Documented proposal requirements and the process for evaluating proposals.

Define Proposal Requirements

Most outsourced work relies on evaluation of the submissions made by potential suppliers. Whether they are called *proposals,* bids, quotations, or something else, you must carefully define both the information that the responders need to analyze and what you expect them to submit.

Based on **procurement planning,** document the *statement of work* (SOW) that you intend to have performed by another party. Include any performance or measurement requirements, acceptance and testing criteria, interface specifications, standards to be followed, deadlines, and any other essential information.

Document all of the information you require in a proposal, being as clear and specific as possible. Cover such areas as:

➤ The details of a proposed solution

➤ All fees and pricing information

➤ Schedule dates

➤ Staffing and expertise

➤ Equipment and facility capabilities (if relevant)

➤ Related experience and references

Determine Your Process for Evaluation

Define an objective basis for **decision making.** Determine important *criteria* for selecting a supplier, such as cost, experience, and price. Prioritize the decision criteria and quantify how you plan to evaluate each proposal regarding each one.

Identify *who will be involved* with the evaluation of proposals, and determine who will ultimately be responsible for the decision. Document your evaluation process, review it with the decision makers, and get their support to proceed.

Write an RFP

Collect all the information that potential suppliers will need into a comprehensive *request for proposal* (RFP). Some other names for a solicitation document include "invitation to bid" or "request for quotation." Whatever it is called, the document includes:

➤ The due date for proposal submission and your schedule for a decision

➤ A SOW consistent with your **scope planning** and project timing

➤ All of the required information expected in a complete proposal

➤ Contact information for any questions or related communication (generally the contact will be you, or someone on your team)

➤ Presentations, bidder conferences, or other meetings (if any)

In preparing an RFP, take full advantage of any guidelines, procedures, forms, or other available reference materials. Before finalizing the document, *have it reviewed* by legal, purchasing, personnel, procurement, or other specialists in your organization who have expertise in outsourcing to ensure that it is consistent with organizational and other requirements and regulations.

90 Source Selection (PMBOK® 12.4)

WHAT: Determining the most appropriate supplier based on submitted proposals and finalizing a contract for the work.

WHEN: Project initiation and planning.

RESULTS: A contract incorporating the requirements of your project, signed by a supplier who can be expected to successfully deliver what you need.

Check the Proposals

Log in each proposal (or bid, or quotation) resulting from your **solicitation.** Review each one to determine that it is *complete and consistent* with the requirements of your request for proposal (RFP). If your bidding process involves presentations or meetings with the bidders, schedule and hold them.

If necessary, request additional or clarifying information for any proposals that have minor defects. *Screen out* any proposals that fail to meet specific stated RFP requirements. If there are too few complete proposals (a typical minimum is three), determine how to proceed. Possible options include:

➤ Evaluating what you do have

➤ Extending the time and solicit more responses

➤ Deciding not to outsource the work

Evaluate the Proposals

If you have a large number of complete proposals, create a *short list* of three to six by reading through all of them quickly and selecting the ones that seem most credible and appropriate.

Follow up on *references* provided and evaluate any work samples submitted with the proposal. Use the quality of the proposal itself to judge the thoroughness and care the bidders bring to their work. Document any personal experience you have with each bidder.

Use a systematic **decision-making** process to sequence the proposals. Schedule sufficient time to *adequately examine each submission*. Determine how well each meets your pre-established evaluation criteria, and use your prioritized criterion weights to rank-order the proposals. Examine the top proposals for overall cost and reasonability. If the sequencing seems "wrong," it may indicate that the inputs to the decision process are faulty. You may need to revisit your criteria, weightings, and evaluations to make the best decision.

Contact the Finalist(s)

Before finalizing the selection, contact each bidder you are considering and *discuss the details* of the proposal with at least one person who would be involved with the work. Use the discussion to assess whether you will be able to establish an effective working relationship, and to ensure that the bidder understands what is required.

Negotiate and Sign the Contract

Pick the proposal that best meets your project's needs, and finalize the selection by involving individuals on both sides who are empowered to enter into a binding legal agreement.

Negotiating contracts (or purchase orders, subcontracts, memos of understanding, or other agreements) for projects requires setting *terms and conditions* aligned with project work. Document what you agree to in a formal contract and describe all responsibilities in the contract by name. Include incentives and penalties based on performance when necessary, and use pre-established contracting forms whenever possible to comply with your organization's standards and to simplify and shorten the approval process.

Check the contract for an unambiguous statement of work (SOW) that defines all milestones and metrics and includes clear process for managing changes. If the contract is not fixed-price, it is especially important to set a "not-to-exceed" limit that will guard against runaway costs and trigger reexamination of the contract when necessary. Have the contract reviewed for problems by experts within your organization, and fix the contract as needed before anyone signs it.

Before signing any contract, thoroughly discuss the terms and conditions to ensure that all parties have a clear and consistent understanding of what the contract states. *Sign the contract* and put it into force.

91 Sponsorship of Projects

WHAT: Establishing and maintaining management support.

WHEN: Throughout a project.

RESULTS: A fast project start, protection of project resources, prompt decisions, and removal of barriers.

Roles of the Sponsor

Project sponsors have responsibilities throughout projects, not just at the start:

➤ *Initiation*—Committing resources, providing data, getting work started

➤ *Planning support*—Providing guidance, validating plans

➤ *Execution support*—Making decisions, solving problems

INITIATION

Sponsors select projects, but they may not provide needed information. If the **project objective** is unclear, or the **project charter** is incomplete or missing, you must fill the gaps. Find out from the sponsor *why the project is being undertaken.*

Work with the sponsor to *identify key stakeholders* for the project who depend upon its successful completion. Verify that **project infrastructure** decisions for reporting and **communications planning** satisfy sponsor and stakeholder expectations.

Verify the initial *resource commitments* for the project, for staffing, funding, equipment, travel, training, and any other identified expenses.

Get approval from the sponsor to hold a project **start-up workshop** to get the project off to a *fast, effective start.* Involve the sponsor in the workshop if possible, either at the start or at the end.

Following initial analysis of the project data and **scope planning,** *check your understanding* of the project with the sponsor by validating the **scope statement** and **project priorities.**

Project sponsorship can be time consuming. Sponsors who begin more than six projects, even if they are small, will probably fail to support adequately at least one of them. Discuss responsibilities throughout the project and *get commitment for ongoing support* from your sponsor.

PLANNING

Throughout **project plan development,** *keep the sponsor informed* (but not necessarily involved) with your progress.

As planning continues, *consult with the sponsor* as necessary to get guidance for **decision making** and for managing trade-offs during **constraint management and plan optimization.**

Establish procedures during the planning process for **problem escalation, scope change management,** and other practices for project control. *Verify support for control processes* with the sponsor and document them.

At the close of planning, assemble your planning documents. If your best plan falls short of the sponsor's desired objective, also document two or more realistic alternatives and use these data to **negotiate project changes** with your sponsor. *Validate an acceptable plan,* freeze the scope specifications, and complete **project baseline setting.**

EXECUTION

Communicate *summary-level project information* to the sponsor frequently. Provide **performance reporting** promptly and factually, even if it contains bad news. Meet with the sponsor regularly to discuss the overall progress of the work and to keep the project visible.

When any aspect of **integrated change control** represents *impact to the project objective,* involve the sponsor in evaluating options and making decisions.

Whenever project progress stalls waiting for a sponsor response to a **problem escalation** or a necessary approval or decision, *set due dates and communicate consequences* of any continued delays. If necessary, delegate ownership upward and track the status in your project status reports.

Whenever a *sponsor will be unavailable* for more than a few days, locate a named individual who has decision and signature authority to ensure continuity.

Loss of Project Sponsorship

If you lose your sponsor (through job change, health problem, resignation, or retirement), *find a new sponsor.* Document the value of your project and the consequences of failure to convince an appropriate high-level individual to support your project. Possible candidates include people who will suffer consequences if your project fails and managers who could (and might) cancel your project.

92 Staff Acquisition (PMBOK® 9.2)

WHAT: Obtaining project staff required to complete project work.

WHEN: Project planning.

RESULTS: A directory of project team members including relevant information, supported by credible commitments.

Existing Staff

As part of **project initiation,** most (or perhaps all) of the project team may be assigned and committed. **Organizational planning** may also identify needs for additional staff. Document the *known staffing needs.*

Identify Any Additional Staffing Gaps

During **resource planning,** identify the project's *unmet needs:*

➤ Missing skills

➤ Required unstaffed roles

➤ Portions of the project with resource overcommitments

Document the needs, with supporting data on project timing, costs, and other consequences of not resolving the staffing shortfall.

Resolve Gaps

Use existing organizational procedures and resources to fill out your project team through reassignment of *internal resources* whenever possible.

If there are still remaining staffing issues, develop a *staffing plan* to resolve them through:

➤ Negotiating increased commitments from part-time team members

➤ **Team development** of existing staff to build new skills

➤ **Procurement planning** and external **source selection** to outsource work

➤ Recruiting and hiring additional staff

➤ Other methods for obtaining additional staff

If you *cannot add needed staff* in a timely manner, **negotiate project changes** to scope or timing that are consistent with the resources you have. Rely on planned overtime only as a last resort, and if you must do it, add it as a significant resource risk during **risk identification.**

Document

Update the *project roster* to add all new project team members, along with their roles and responsibilities.

93 Start-up Workshop

WHAT: A meeting to initiate project efforts and to build teamwork.

WHEN: Project planning or project execution (or both).

RESULTS: Consistent understanding of project goals and plans, a quick start on the work, and a cohesive project team.

Project start-up workshops go by *other names,* including project kick-offs, project initiation meetings, project planning workshops, and project launches.

Prepare

Justify the project start-up workshop by outlining the benefits you expect to achieve. One primary benefit of a face-to-face meeting is establishing **teamwork** and trust on the project team. For global teams and other virtual teams, it is often the difference between project success and disaster. Additional benefits include unambiguous understanding of the project, a fast and efficient project beginning, collaborative initial **project plan development,** and team **motivation.** With these benefits come costs—for travel, time, and other investments. Build the business case for a workshop and get approval to conduct one.

Prior to the workshop, assemble the *project documents* you will use, including the **project objective, project charter, user needs assessments,** your **project infrastructure** decisions, and any other project and **scope planning** documents available.

Develop an *agenda* to support your workshop objectives. The length and content of the agenda will vary depending on the type and size of the project, but allow a minimum of a half day, even for short projects. Significant programs may require a series of multi-day workshops. Begin the agenda with introductions and a review of project expectations. Allow sufficient time for each major analysis, planning, or other result you need from the workshop. Include time for team-building activities to allow the staff to get to know one another.

Determine who in addition to the core project team should participate, and *schedule the workshop* when they can attend. In advance, obtain commitment from all participants to attend the entire meeting.

Plan the logistics for your **meeting.** You will accomplish more if you get away from workplace interruptions, so reserve a suitable off-site location. Arrange the room for a productive workshop, and bring any supplies you will need such as pens, tape, flipcharts, and yellow sticky notes. While it is possible to facilitate your own workshop, getting another person to lead the meeting will allow you to contribute and participate more fully.

Meet

Begin with *introductions* and let people interact with each other. Clarify each person's contribution to the team. Spend some time reviewing the agenda and objectives for the workshop, and discuss the project (with the sponsor if possible) to ensure that everyone understands the goals.

During the workshop, use a flip-chart to *capture data:* issues, relevant assumptions, decisions, plans, and action items. Use the workshop to build on the foundation of information available. Work to understand the **project priorities,** and to improve the **scope planning** using "Is/Is not" analysis on the project deliverables. If the planning process has begun, review the work breakdown structure from **scope definition** and focus on **activity duration estimates, schedule development, resource analysis,** and **risk identification.**

Include activities in the workshop where people work together in pairs or small groups for *team building,* and use collaborative processes such as **brainstorming** and **creative problem solving.** Have some fun during the workshop.

Wrap up the workshop by reviewing what you have accomplished and identifying the next steps. Assign an owner and a due date for all action items and tasks. End by renewing team commitments and thanking all participants.

Follow Up

Document the results of the workshop, and distribute the information to the team and appropriate stakeholders. Discuss workshop results with your sponsor.

Follow up on all action items and unfinished business of the workshop.

If you are using a **software tool for project management,** enter the results of the workshop into the database. Continue the *planning process* to develop the remaining data needed for **project baseline setting.**

94 **Status Collection**

WHAT: Periodic collection of project activity information.

WHEN: Project execution and control.

RESULTS: Timely, accurate progress data and early detection of problems.

Methods

Determining project status is primarily the responsibility of the *project leader.* The process for status collection is a key part of **communications planning,** and it is central to **project plan execution.** Status collection begins the project tracking cycle.

Decisions regarding status collection are part of **project infrastructure** planning. There are many ways to *collect the data,* although most people prefer to do it in writing to minimize confusion and to retain a tangible account. Typical methods include:

➤ E-mail

➤ Paper or on-line forms

➤ Using the services of a **project office**

➤ One-on-one meetings

➤ Telephone conversations

➤ Project team meetings

Use a method that works for you, and make collection as *simple* as practical. On most projects people are very busy, so if the process is complicated or time consuming, you will not get the information you need.

The *frequency* of data collection also varies, but most status collection is done weekly. Collecting information less often reduces **schedule control.**

What to Collect

Project status information is of two *type*s: hard data (facts and figures) and soft data (anecdotal information, rumors, and less specific information). Both types of status are useful. **Plan variance analysis,** project control, and **performance reporting** all depend on hard data. Soft status information reveals root causes of current problems and can provide early warning of potential project risks.

Hard status data include all the **project diagnostic metrics** that you are tracking. This encompasses all of the metrics used for **earned value management.**

Schedule and resource metrics are collected routinely every status cycle, with scope and other metrics collected as necessary. Typical hard data examples are:

➤ Activities completed or delayed

➤ Actual activity start and finish dates

➤ Duration adjustments for incomplete activities

➤ Milestones completed or missed

➤ Actual activity effort and cost data

➤ Effort adjustments for incomplete activities

➤ Data regarding specification changes

➤ Results of deliverable tests

You will also uncover less tangible information, both during status collection and during informal communications. This *soft project status* includes information such as:

➤ Priority conflicts arising from expected new projects or other work

➤ Productivity problems of team members

➤ Potential changes to the project environment

➤ Rumored delay of required project inputs

➤ Problem situations that have a common root cause

➤ Conflicts requiring more authority to resolve than you have

➤ Delayed resolution of **problem escalations**

Pitfalls

There are many *common problems* that can result in inadequate status information. Good practices for avoiding these include:

➤ Do not "shoot the messenger" who brings bad news. When team members are criticized or punished for negative news, they stop providing any useful information.

➤ Always collect the status data, every cycle. Good, timely information is even more important during times of high stress and significant problems.

➤ Acknowledge and use the information you collect. If it looks like you do not care about the information received, your team members will stop providing it. Make use of status data from all contributors in your **information distribution.**

➤ Work hard to get status data from distant team members on **global teams** and from external contributors. Be persistent, make multiple requests when necessary, contact them when they are at work (regardless of the time where you are), and verify the data.

➤ Listen actively. Paraphrase what you are told to ensure that you understood what was said. Ask open questions that require more than a yes or no answer, and probe for the root causes that underlie the status.

95 Team Development (PMBOK® 9.3)

WHAT: Ensuring that the project staff builds required skills and functions well as a team.

WHEN: Throughout a project.

RESULTS: A cooperative, effective team capable of completing the project.

Identify the Skills the Project Requires

As a project leader, be constantly on the alert for opportunities on the team to build *new skills.* Encouraging team members to develop their skills increases **motivation** and can provide the project with staffing options not available when a team is dependent on a single individual with unique talents.

Based on the project's **resource planning** and **required skills analysis,** identify any *needed skills* that no one on the team possesses. For skills that you are unable to add through **staff acquisition,** look for team members who may be willing and able candidates for learning new skills.

Another place where skill gaps can surface is **performance problem resolution.** Some *missed commitments* are a consequence of team members who lack necessary skills.

Be aware that **scope change control** and other *project shifts* may also generate new project activities that no one currently on the team knows how to do.

Build New Skills

Acquiring *new skills* on the team can be done through:

➤ Allowing people to get training

➤ **Coaching and mentoring**

➤ Networking with others

➤ Self-development

Build an Effective Project Team

Team effectiveness is also enhanced through **teamwork building and maintenance.** *Co-location,* even for short periods, helps in avoiding trouble and in **conflict resolution.** Even for global teams, periodic face-to-face meetings are essential for building relationships and trust that a team depends upon in times of project difficulty.

Positive feedback also builds team cohesion, whether through personal thanks, specific mentions of project contributions in **performance reporting,** or through other **rewards and recognition.**

96 Teamwork Building and Maintenance

WHAT: Establishing and maintaining team cooperation, engagement, and trust.

WHEN: Throughout a project.

RESULTS: Less conflict and chaos, and faster, less expensive projects.

Create a Good Foundation

Define the *objectives* for the team in very specific terms. Involve everyone in **user needs assessment** for the project, and verify that the team understands the **project objective** and **project vision.**

Staff the team with capable people with the talents identified in your **required skills analysis.** Clearly identify the *roles and responsibilities* for each team member, and focus **staff acquisition** efforts on finding individuals with good interpersonal skills, general knowledge, and no conflicting priorities.

Work to understand the team members, and determine the best *leadership style* for the group. Use your experience and knowledge of the people to strike an appropriate **leadership** balance between consensus management and autocratic control.

Structure how the team will work effectively. Determine a **project infrastructure** that facilitates team productivity, and ensure effective information flow through **communications planning.** Identify and work to minimize any unnecessary overhead.

Teamwork emerges most easily through proximity, so if it is possible, *co-locate* the team where members can work together permanently throughout the project. If co-location is not possible, schedule face-to-face meetings periodically, at least for portions of the team, and use technology to enhance **virtual team** communication.

Build the Team

Begin team building through a project **start-up workshop.** Develop trust and interpersonal relationships through team-building activities, and make connections within the team using pair and group interactions.

Align the objectives of the project with individual goals. Build **motivation** by identifying "What's in it for me?" for each person on the team, and respect individual preferences when **delegating responsibility.**

Especially on crossfunctional or **matrix teams,** encourage good team *working relationships.* Foster one-on-one and small group interactions. Get to know new team members quickly, and identify common interests, experiences, education, or background.

Establish honest, *open communication*. In **global team communication,** be sensitive to different preferences and time differences. Choose technical tools that are acceptable to all, and shift conference call schedules periodically to share time zone inconveniences. **Global team work styles** also vary, so adjust project plans to minimize potential project impact.

When *conflicts* arise, deal with differences promptly in a constructive, nonjudgmental environment. Use **conflict resolution** as an opportunity to learn, to improve the project, and to build mutual respect within the team.

Maintain Team Relationships

Meet face-to-face regularly, at least twice a year even for global teams. Renew and reinforce interpersonal relationships. Establish a team identity or name that brings the team together.

Be disciplined in your *project communications.* Monitor project progress through frequent **status collection, plan variance analysis,** and **performance reporting.** In addition to formal communication, **communicate informally** with the team regularly, and encourage informal interaction among the team members.

Demonstrate *loyalty* to the team and praise team members who help each other or fill in when others are absent. Find frequent opportunities to thank people for their accomplishments and take full advantage of programs for **rewards and recognition.**

Confront and resolve issues, *barriers to progress,* and problems quickly. Seek team members' participation in all **decision making** that involves them. Use team analysis and **creative problem solving** to resolve difficulties within the team whenever possible. When team members fail to meet commitments, work on **performance problem resolution** with them individually. For situations that are beyond your authority, seek rapid resolution through **problem escalation.**

Encourage *fun and humor.* Periodically schedule events, chosen by the team, to get the team together outside the project. Find opportunities as a team to eat together; food is something everyone has in common and is very effective in connecting people.

97 Time Management

WHAT: Improving your efficiency and getting results sooner.

WHEN: Throughout a project.

RESULTS: Lower stress, better performance, and faster achievement of important outcomes.

Document and Prioritize Activities

On a *single list,* capture all your tasks and activities. If you use a paper list, maintain it as long as possible on the same sheet by adding new items at the bottom and drawing a single line through completed tasks. Rewrite the list only when you run out of space or the majority of the list is crossed out. If you maintain your list electronically, ensure that open items are rolled forward day by day. With each listed item, provide a space for:

➤ A clear item description, including the deliverable(s)

➤ Priority of the work

➤ Expected start and target completion

➤ Actual completion date

Assign a priority to each listed item. Mark time critical and most important items "A" or "High." For necessary but less critical work, assign a "B" or "Medium" priority. Indicate lowest priority for everything else on your action list using "C" or "Low." Set priorities based on the value of the results, not just apparent urgency. Following project or organizational changes, review your priorities.

Examine each item on the list and eliminate any of the lowest priority items that you can safely exclude. Further *reduce your list* by **delegating responsibility** for listed items to other people who could be responsible for the work. Attend only the **meetings** you must, and encourage the meeting leaders to shorten them, end on time, and cancel them whenever they serve no compelling business reason.

Whether your list is on paper or electronic, *maintain a log* of the items you finish with a completion date for reporting and future reference.

Plan Your Time

For any long-term goals, do something each week that contributes to the goal. Use the principles of **scope definition** to *decompose large objectives* into smaller parts using a work breakdown structure.

First, schedule all the *highest priority* "A" items into your calendar. Then schedule as many "B" priority items as will fit, but plan for the unexpected by not packing every minute of each day. Plan to work on "C" priority items only when you have completed all higher priority work.

Review your plans for the next day as your final daily task. Adjust your schedule to include any unfinished items. Cross off all the items you have finished, noting the completion date. Use **schedule control** to manage your time.

Schedule work that requires concentration or large blocks of uninterrupted time first. Do what you need to do to create blocks of time without meetings or distractions where you can *focus* on these goals.

Plan all *meetings* you are responsible for by setting a precise agenda. Minimize time overrun by scheduling meetings just before lunch, at the end of the day, or with some other natural limit. End your meetings early whenever possible.

Work Effectively

➤ *Avoid* unproductive meetings.

➤ Persevere—*finish* what you start.

➤ Don't *procrastinate.*

➤ *Say "no"* when you must to preserve your objectives.

➤ *Set time limits* for telephone calls and diplomatically end them on time.

➤ Dispatch forms efficiently—*handle papers only once.*

➤ *Scan and delete* trivial email quickly, and file—*don't print*—other e-mail.

➤ Work on *difficult things* during the most productive parts of your day.

➤ Take *breaks.*

➤ Use a *Do Not Disturb* sign.

➤ Do your work and *go home*—long hours are often not productive hours.

98 Transitioning to Project Leadership

WHAT: Understanding the changes required when moving from a project contributor to leader.

WHEN: As necessary.

RESULTS: A quick and successful transition into a project leadership role.

Contrasts

The daily work of a project leader differs in many ways from the work of other project team members:

Project team members	Project leaders
➤ Seek the best solutions	➤ Seek practical solutions
➤ Work mostly with "things"	➤ Work mostly with people
➤ Need deep, specialized expertise	➤ Need broad, general knowledge
➤ Are evaluated on personal work	➤ Are evaluated on the work of others
➤ Focus on individual goals	➤ Focus on team and overall goals

The transition to a project leadership role can be very difficult and frustrating because the jobs are so different, and new leaders are often reluctant to give up technical and execution responsibility. Because project leaders need to allocate about 10 percent of their time for each core project team member, any project leader with a sizable team who retains significant technical responsibilities is responsible for *two full-time jobs.*

Communication

One of the most important responsibilities of the project leader is *information management:* **status collection, information distribution,** and **performance reporting.** Project leaders need to be conduits for formal project communication, not barriers. Good leaders become adept at summarizing, filtering, and transferring clear data up (to management and sponsors), down (to contributors), and laterally (to leaders of related projects). In addition, effective project leaders devote substantial effort to **informal communication** throughout the project.

Most project leaders attend many *meetings,* so **meeting preparation** and **meeting execution** skills are crucial for minimizing the time invested and maximizing meeting value.

Leading and Motivating

Project leaders need to be *people-oriented.* They need to understand their project teams to determine what **leadership** styles will work best. **Delegating responsibility** for project activities to team members requires a facility for building **teamwork** and **motivation.** Getting people from other organizations to cooperate depends on exerting **influence without authority.** Project leaders also provide **coaching and mentoring** for team members, and they must take advantage of opportunities for **team development.**

Project leaders need to keep a *systems view* and focus on the overall objectives. They also need to develop their ability to multi-task, working effectively through frequent interruptions.

Planning

Project plan development is a very visible responsibility of any project leader. In addition to leading the **scope definition, schedule development, resource planning,** and other effort, the project leader is responsible for documenting the plans and determining how to store the information. The project leader must become proficient at using **software tools for project management.** The leader is also responsible for **negotiating project changes** that are necessary to ensure a realistic *baseline project plan.*

Business Focus

Project leaders need to understand the project **user needs assessment** and the perspective of the sponsor and other project stakeholders. *Project finances* and **cost budgeting** are essential to the overall success of the project.

99 User Needs Assessment

WHAT: Understanding what users of your project outputs require and will accept.

WHEN: Project initiation and planning.

RESULTS: Project deliverables that meet needs and deliver business value.

Organize and Set Objectives

User needs information emerges from **project initiation**, but you rarely begin with sufficient data. Potentially, users are all the people who can interact with the project deliverable(s), including:

➤ People who use it to do their jobs

➤ People who buy or pay for it

➤ People who deliver, install, or maintain it

➤ Deliverable approvers

➤ Managers of any of these people

User needs may be either *stated or unstated.* Stated needs are generally the easiest to uncover, and they relate to features and performance. Unstated needs include basic needs (requirements that may be taken for granted by most users) and "excitement" needs, which may be based on new technology or ideas that are not familiar to most users. Documenting all the needs requires observation, research, creativity, and imagination.

Identify the user information necessary for **scope planning** that is not available. For any missing information, frame clear, specific questions that must be answered, and decide in advance how you will apply the information (regardless of what you learn). *Set objectives* and plan the activities required to achieve them.

Project teams may lack skills required for thorough assessment of user needs, requiring *assistance* from specialists experienced in product management or marketing. Identify any crossfunctional talent and outside resources that may be required. Even if you are not directly involved in collecting user information, ensure that staff from your core project team is at least involved setting objectives at the start and in analyzing and summarizing the results at the end.

User assessment may require significant time and effort. If so, obtain necessary funding and *management commitment* in advance.

Identify What You Know

Review *available user information.* Strategic planning at the organization level generally summarizes information on customers and users. Look for any relevant other research or publicly published data.

Document what you know about user needs based on existing data.

Resolve Unmet Information Needs

Determine *additional information* you require. For projects that develop products or services to be sold, plan for **market research**. For projects having a predefined finite number of users, plan and schedule **customer interviews**.

Work to *creatively understand opportunities* for new technology or ideas, and test alternative options and combinations of concepts.

Document and Use the Data

Summarize user needs information and discuss it with your project sponsor, the team, and other stakeholders. Determine what the information means for the project and use it to complete your scope planning. Consider user data in setting **project priorities** and managing **scope change control**.

For longer projects, revisit the user needs assessment during each **project review**, and as needed as part of **integrated change control**.

100 **Virtual Teams – Technical Tools**

WHAT: Using technology to assist in managing distributed teams.

WHEN: Throughout a project.

RESULTS: Effective long-distance collaboration and sharing of project information.

Tools for Communications

In **communications planning,** *prepare in advance* for any technological tools you will use. Set expectations for timing, and establish standard formats for **performance reporting** and other written project communications. For **global team communications,** adopt tools and techniques that all of the team can and will use effectively. With careful planning, technical tools can increase your **influence without authority.**

For **meetings,** *teleconferencing* is the most common tool. Telephones, videoconferencing, and computer networking methods can all be effective. Specialized media rooms set up for videoconferencing and Web-based meetings are particularly useful when participants need to share images, graphics, software applications, live video, or other complex visual information.

Good teleconferencing (like any meeting) requires *advance planning.* Set an agenda before the meeting with topics, owners, timing, and expected outcomes for each item the meeting will address. If there will not be easy access to images during the teleconference, send visual information in advance via e-mail, FAX, or express mail, or place files on websites that all will be able to access. When dealing with significant time differences, schedule meetings at a time that is as mutually convenient as possible. Schedule meetings so that all participants will be able to meet during their normal working hours, at least once in a while.

For *technology-assisted meetings,* select technology that all the participants can competently use, and make it part of the **project infrastructure.** Obtain agreement from the entire project team (including any involved external consultants, partners, and outside service suppliers) to use the meeting technology, and test all hardware before use for compatibility. Begin technology-mediated meetings with introductions, and throughout the meeting remind participants to state their names before speaking.

General communications via e-mail and other *computer messaging* technologies are also vital to virtual teams, especially when there are significant time differences. Resolve any issues of access, technical compatibility, and security in advance, so team members can communicate freely. If new software releases are scheduled, give everyone prior warning. Repeat your compatibility tests after any changes or upgrades. Check that attachments to e-mails and files stored on computer networks are accessible using software available to all team members. If some team members have limited or low-speed network access, avoid techniques that require very large files.

Always *reread all e-mails* and other written communications before sending them to check for clarity, tone, and terminology. As you review what you have written, think how you would react to it if you received it. Encourage frequent, short communications.

Whenever complex information needs to be shared across the team, communicate it in *several ways*. If information distribution is initially verbal, follow up with a written summary. Tailor your communication to the recipients, and offer to follow up and discuss any written communication that may be unclear.

Work Tools

As with communication tools, check file sharing and *collaboration tools* that your project will need in advance for compatibility and performance. Using Web-based tools, E-rooms, instant messaging, file servers, **software tools for project management,** and other distance collaboration tools can be very effective in technical projects if their use is carefully planned and aligned with project requirements.

Combine High-Tech with "High Touch"

Technology and other capabilities are essential throughout **project plan execution,** but must be *in addition to,* not instead of, other types of communication. High technology communication works best when accompanied by other "high-touch," more personal methods. Use all available tools, but avoid misuse. Voice-mail can be extremely valuable for **communicating informally** when team members share a language and culture, but for team members who speak different languages, voice-mail can be easily misinterpreted and may seem rude or impolite.

Never miss an opportunity for *one-on-one meetings* to build **teamwork** and trust, even when it is not with the entire team. Get the whole team together as frequently as practical, at least semiannually, for events such as project **start-up workshops, project plan development,** and **project reviews.**

Exchanging photographs between distant locations, particularly informal pictures of team members outside of the workplace, is an effective way to build personal connections on a virtual team.

Index

Index

Communication process (*cont.*)
  presentations, 100–101
  project charter, 111–112
  status collection, 207–209
  and virtual teams, 220–221
Confidentiality
  and communications plan, 20
  and mentoring, 16
Conflict
  avoidance tactics, 21
  sources of, 21
Conflict resolution, 21–22
  forcing solution, 21, 22
  methods, 21–22
Consensus building
  Delphi technique, 46–47
  process of, 23–24
Constraint management, 25–27, 32
Contracts
  administration of, 28–29, 85
  closeout of, 30
  negotiation of, 84–85, 200
  statement of work (SOW), 200
  termination of project, 8–9
Control process
  cause-and-effect analysis, 14–15
  earned value management (EVM), 48–50
  integrated change control, 60–62
  negotiation of project changes, 86–87
  plan variance analysis, 98–99
  problem escalation, 102–103
  project metrics, diagnostic, 119–120
  project metrics, predictive, 121–122
  project metrics, retrospective, 123–124
  project metrics, selection and implementation, 125–127
  review of project, 139–141
Cost estimation, 35–37
  duration estimates, 35–36
  in earned value management (EVM), 48–49
  effort estimates, 35
  uncertainty, adjustment for, 36

Cost process
  budgeting, 31–32
  cost control, 33–34
  cost impact, 154
  cost performance (CP), calculation of, 49
  cost performance index (CPI), calculation of, 49–50
  estimation of costs, 35–37
  resource planning, 160–161
  return on investment analysis, 164–165
Creative problem solving, 34, 38–39, 42
Critical path methodology (CPM), 180–181
Crosscultural communication, 51–52
Crosscultural work styles, 53–54
Crossfunctional teams, 69–70
Customer interviews, 40–41, 67
Customer requirements, quality planning, 151

D
Decision making
  brainstorming, 10–11, 42
  cause-and-effect analysis, 42
  changes to projects, 61–62
  creative problem solving, 38–39, 42
  and Delphi technique, 46–47
  infrastructure decisions list, 113–115
  market research, 67–68
  problem escalation, 102–103
  process of, 42–43
Delegation, 44–45
  and principle of reciprocity, 56
  and problem escalation, 102–103
Delphi technique, 46–47
Dependency diagrams, 7
Dependent projects. *See* Multiple dependent projects
Diagnostic project metrics, 119–120
Discounted payback, ROI analysis, 165
Documentation
  activity definition, 1–2
  of communications decisions, 20

Information distribution, 58–59
  global teams, 52
  project management information
    system (PMIS), 59
  routine communications, 58–59
Information management, and
  leader, 216
Infrastructure of project, 113–116
  communications planning, 20
  infrastructure decisions list,
    113–115
  status collection, 207–209
Initiation of project, 117–118
Integrated change control, 60–62
Interface management, multiple
  dependent projects, 79
Internal rate of return, ROI analysis,
  165
Interviews, customer interviews,
  40–41, 67
Ishikawa charts, 14

L
Leadership process
  business focus, 217
  coaching/mentoring, 16–17
  critical leadership skills, 63
  daily routine, example of, 216
  delegation, 44–45
  influence without authority, 55–57,
    63
  information management, 216
  leadership basics, 63–64
  leadership styles, 63–64
  motivating team, 76–77, 217
  organizational change, 88–89
  planning process, 217
  rewards and recognition, 166–
    167
  transitioning to project leadership,
    216–217
Lessons learned, 65–66
  and cancelled projects, 13

M
Management by wandering around
  (MBWA), 18

Market research, 67–68
  qualitative methods, 67
  quantitative methods, 67
Matrix teams, 69–70
  maintaining team, 70
  team building, 69–70
Meetings
  closing, 74–75
  consensus building, 23–24
  execution of, 73–75
  ground rules, 73
  lessons learned analysis, 65–66
  performance problem resolution,
    94–95
  preparation for, 71–72
  roles in, 71–72
  running meeting, 74
  teleconferencing, 20, 72, 220
  time management, 215
Mentoring, 16–17, 64
Metrics. *See* Project metrics
Microsoft Project, 193
Mission, project objectives, 128–129
Monte Carlo simulation, 154
Motivating team, 76–77
  demotivating factors, 77
  and goal setting, 44
  guidelines, 76–77
  rewards and recognition, 26, 77,
    166–167
Multiple dependent projects, 78–80
  activity sequencing, 5–7
  decompose program, 78–79
  integration phase, 80
  interface management, 79
Multiple independent projects, 78–80
  prioritize set of projects, 81
  project objectives, 82

N
Needs assessment, for users, 218–219
Negotiation
  of contracts, 84–85, 200
  project changes, 86–87
Net present value (NPV), ROI
  analysis, 165
Niku Project Workbench, 193